FILMING T. E. LAWRENCE

FILMING
T. E. LAWRENCE:
KORDA'S LOST EPICS

Edited and introduced by

Andrew Kelly, James Pepper
and Jeffrey Richards

I.B. Tauris Publishers

LONDON • NEW YORK

Published in 1997 by I.B. Tauris and Co Ltd
Victoria House, Bloomsbury Square,
London WC1B 4DZ

In the United States of America and in Canada
distributed by St Martin's Press, 175 Fifth Avenue,
New York NY 10010

Introduction and editorial matter copyright © 1997 by Andrew Kelly,
James Pepper and Jeffrey Richards

A full CIP record for this book is available from the British Library

A full CIP record for this book is available from the Library of
Congress

ISBN 1 86064 048 6

Set in Monotype Bembo by Ewan Smith, London

Printed and bound in Great Britain by WBC Ltd, Bridgend,
Mid Glamorgan

CONTENTS

ACKNOWLEDGEMENTS

A number of people have been of great assistance in the production of this book. We would like to thank particularly Philippa Brewster of I.B. Tauris for taking this project on board and for her advice throughout the production process. We would also like to thank Kevin Brownlow. James Chapman discovered and drew our attention to the article by Leslie Howard. We are also very grateful for the research by Jeffrey Hulbert in the Foreign Office records at the Public Record Office. Rachel Phillips and Susan Waddington typed the manuscript with speed and good humour. Special thanks are extended to George Locke who located the Korda/Lawrence screenplay.

We are particularly grateful to Michael Carey of Tweedie and Prideaux Solicitors and Andrew Luff of London Films for their assistance on copyright clearance. Howard Coster's portrait of Lawrence is used by kind permission of the Royal Photographic Society, Bath. Thanks are due to Debbie Ireland for this. The photograph of Lawrence and Liddell Hart is reproduced courtesy of the Trustees of the Liddell Hart Centre for Military Archives, King's College, London. All other stills and portraits are reproduced courtesy of the Stills, Posters and Designs Division of the British Film Institute. The editors have made every attempt to trace copyright holders of this material. If we have missed anyone we should be grateful if you could write to us care of the publishers so that this can be rectified in any future edition.

INTRODUCTION:
FILMING LAWRENCE

The legend of Lawrence of Arabia was created by film. The American journalist Lowell Thomas, who had covered the First World War in the Near East, toured the globe for three years immediately after the war with a lecture and slide show entitled 'With Lawrence in Arabia'. He attracted millions of people to see the 'hitherto unknown story of Lawrence and the war in the land of the Arabian Nights'.[1] This formed the basis of Thomas's book *With Lawrence in Arabia*, published in 1924. When Lawrence's own book *The Seven Pillars of Wisdom* appeared, printed initially in a limited edition in 1926 but then in an abridged popular version called *Revolt in the Desert* in 1927, the legend was complete. Lawrence had been retrospectively imbued with a romantic glamour and turned into what Thomas called him in his book – 'A Modern Arabian Knight'. He had become a warrior hero of empire in the tradition of Havelock and Gordon.

From the outset film adaptations of *Revolt in the Desert* were being mooted. Producer Herbert Wilcox recalled in his autobiography receiving a visit in 1926 from Lawrence and his literary agent Raymond Savage with the idea of a film version of the book. Wilcox found the story 'not good cinema and in spots rather sordid ... I ventured the opinion that I could not see cinema audiences seeking entertainment being attracted to such a subject.'[2]

Other producers were less chary. Hollywood producer-director Rex Ingram, who is best remembered for his enormously influential First World War epic *The Four Horsemen of the Apocalypse* (1921) and its wartime companion piece *Mare Nostrum* (1926), had also made two successful romantic desert films, *The Arab* (1924) and *The Garden of Allah* (1927). One of the original subscribers to the private publication of *The Seven Pillars of Wisdom*, Ingram was perhaps the most qualified film director of the silent era to try to tackle Lawrence's growing legend. In 1927 he gingerly sounded out Lawrence about bringing his memoir to the screen. Lawrence characteristically responded:

> I do not envy you your film job. It must be a very difficult art, an expression of yourself (and of the author of the scenario) at two removes. Indeed I wonder that it is ever so good as it seems to be. They babble sometimes to me of making a film of *Revolt in the Desert*. I have no property in it so that I hope they will not. Hollywood offered £6,000 or something, which the trustees turned down. Long may they go on turning it down. I'd hate to see myself parodied on the pitiful basis of my record of what the fellows with me did.

Ironically, although Ingram did not get the job, his films inspired the man who eventually would, David Lean. Later in life, Lean remarked: 'the man who really got me going was Rex Ingram ... in everything he did the camera-work was impeccable.' In 1929, the British producer M. A. Wetherell, who had directed and starred in the biopic *Livingstone* in 1925, tried and failed to get permission to film *Revolt*.[3]

Then in 1934 Alexander Korda, Britain's premier producer of prestige films, became interested in the project. He was to produce the definitive film versions of Edgar Wallace's *Sanders of the River* (1935), A. E. W. Mason's *The Four Feathers* (1939) and Rudyard Kipling's *The Jungle Book* (1942). A romantic, an Anglophile and an imperialist, Korda saw in the personality and career of T. E. Lawrence, with all the elements of glamour, romance and adventure, a perfect cinematic subject. He managed to secure the film rights to *Revolt in the Desert* in 1934. Lawrence had become anxious that a Hollywood version of his career would be made, inaccurate, sensationalized and with a fictional love interest added. In the contract with Korda, Lawrence's trustees specified that the film-makers must be British, that there should be 'no departure from historical accuracy' and that 'no female characters' should be introduced.[4]

In May 1934 Korda announced that Leslie Howard would play the lead in the forthcoming film, with Lewis Milestone, who had directed the celebrated First World War film *All Quiet on the Western Front*, directing.[5] Korda also had discussions with Captain Basil Liddell Hart, biographer and friend of Lawrence, about using his biography to flesh out some of the details in *Revolt*. But once again Lawrence got cold feet and asked Korda not to proceed with the film during his lifetime. Korda agreed. Lawrence said he found Korda 'quite unexpectedly sensitive' to 'the inconveniences his proposed film of *Revolt* would set in my path'.[6]

But the situation changed dramatically with Lawrence's death following a motorcycle accident in May 1935. His premature death completed Lawrence's heroic apotheosis. *The Seven Pillars of Wisdom* was produced in a posthumous popular edition, and Ace Films made a 36-minute documentary, *Lawrence of Arabia*, largely based on still photographs in the collection of the Imperial War Museum. In the circumstances, the Lawrence trustees gave Korda permission to go ahead with his feature film.[7] Thus began a four-year saga, ending not in the production of the envisaged epic but in the abandonment of the project.

Both artistic and financial problems beset the production along the way, but its fate seems to have been determined ultimately by politically inspired censorship.[8] The plan was for parts of the film to be shot on location in Palestine and Transjordan, for which the co-operation of the Colonial Office would be necessary. Lt.-Col. W. F. Stirling DSO, MC, who had been governor of Jaffa between 1920 and 1923, was engaged as technical and military adviser and charged with approaching the Colonial Office.

On 17 July 1935, Stirling had an interview with K. W. Blaxter at the Colonial Office. Colonel Stirling explained that all the locations would be shot in Palestine and Transjordan, that they would want to stage camel charges and bombing raids, that they planned to enlist local tribesmen as extras and that there would be no scenes set in Mecca or the Holy Places. But Blaxter noted: 'they apparently will want to show certain episodes of the Turks in retreat and also in order to lead up to the reasons for the Arab revolt to show certain occurrences in which the Turks behaved in an unfavourable light. For example he mentioned certain hangings which were carried out on instructions from Turkish commanders.' Blaxter said that the best course would be for the Colonial Office to communicate with the authorities in Jerusalem, telling them what the proposals were and asking if they or the Transjordan government had any objections. But since the film also involved the Turks, he advised Stirling to consult the Foreign Office.[9]

Stirling called on G. W. Rendel, head of the Eastern Department of the Foreign Office, on 22 July 1935, and Rendel reported to Blaxter:

> We see no general objections to this proposal. The inevitable scenes of Turkish cruelty may, however, need a little vetting, and I think we should ask for an opportunity of criticizing the

passages dealing with the Arab revolt and especially the passages (if any) which deal with HMG's alleged promises to King Hussein.[10]

This was duly minuted as Foreign Office policy. The authorities in Palestine and Transjordan raised no objection and agreed to provide facilities, although H. L. Baggallay, clerk in the Eastern Department of the Foreign Office, submitted a memorandum urging that no battle scenes be staged near the Hejaz frontier:

> It would be possible ... to explain beforehand to the Saudi Government what was going to happen, but we know by experience that it takes a very long time for instructions to travel from the central government to their outlying governors and police posts, and in any case are inclined to doubt whether the probably illiterate commandant of some Saudi post on the frontier would be able to take in the explanation that what looked like a battle was really a piece of acting.

In return for this cooperation, Stirling agreed that the finished film should be shown to both the Foreign Office and the Colonial Office for their comments.[11]

In January 1936, Alexander Korda announced the inclusion of the film of *Revolt in the Desert* in his schedule for the coming year.[12] Zoltan Korda, Alexander's brother and the director of Korda's imperial trilogy *Sanders of the River*, *The Drum* and *The Four Feathers*, would direct and the script would be by John Monk Saunders. Saunders, an American, had been a First World War combat pilot and Rhodes scholar, and subsequently a Hollywood scriptwriter specializing in aerial epics (*The Eagle and the Hawk*, *Wings*, *Ace of Aces*). He won an Academy Award for writing *The Dawn Patrol* (1930). His script for *Revolt in the Desert* was approved by the Lawrence Trustees on 29 December 1936. The leading role would be played by Walter Hudd, a character actor who resembled Lawrence facially and who had played the Lawrence-inspired character

Private Meek in George Bernard Shaw's play *Too True To Be Good*. Lawrence himself had recommended Hudd for the role in early discussions about filming. Raymond Massey was invited to play Feisal.[13] For much of 1936, however, Palestine was in the grip of serious disorder as the Arabs mounted a campaign to drive out the British, which included a general strike, attacks on trains and motor vehicle convoys and murder. This must account for the further delay to Korda's production.

When the project was resurrected early in 1937, a new team was responsible. Saunders had been reassigned to script Korda's ambitious drama-documentary *Conquest of the Air*. Miles Malleson had completed a new script and Brian Desmond Hurst had been assigned to direct. Malleson, an actor and playwright, had been a prominent pacifist during the First World War but went on to script such imperial epics as *Rhodes of Africa* (1936), *Victoria the Great* (1937) and *Sixty Glorious Years* (1938). Hurst was a Northern Irishman who could speak Arabic and had directed several films for Associated British Pictures (*Ourselves Alone, Glamorous Night, Sensation*) before being signed by Korda. Hurst and Duncan Guthrie prepared a shooting script from the Malleson scenario. Korda tested John Clements for the role of Lawrence and offered it to him,[14] but, according to Clements, subsequently changed his mind and successively declared his intention of casting Clifford Evans, Robert Donat, Leslie Howard and Laurence Olivier. Hurst was about to leave on a trip to Jerusalem to scout locations when Korda cancelled the trip, saying that the Palestine government refused to permit large gatherings of Arabs and they could not make the film without crowds of Arab extras.[15]

Shortly thereafter Korda, experiencing one of his periodic cash crises, disposed of the Lawrence project to another company, New World Films, which was based at Denham Studios and would use Korda's production facilities. They announced that Harold Schuster would direct and the American camera-man James Wong Howe would photograph the film.[16] Colonel Stirling continued in his capacity as military adviser. On 4 March 1937, the Colonial Office telegraphed the Palestine government to say that New World Films were ready to fly out two film units to shoot location sequences in Palestine and Transjordan and that they hoped to complete their work by 15 May. The Palestine government cabled back that they had no objection under the present circumstances, but that it must be understood that if the situation seriously deteriorated, the work might have to be suspended.[17] In fact the film units never left. There were apparently problems over the script. Sir Edward Villiers, chairman of New World, said later that 'several scripts had been written, none has yet proved entirely satisfactory. In fact each seemed to be worse than the last, as more Hollywood influence … seemed to permeate each successive attempt. These and other difficulties had so far rendered it impossible to start taking the scenes.'[18]

During the summer, Korda reacquired the rights to the project, reactivated the Malleson script, rechristened it *Lawrence of Arabia* and announced in October 1937 that Leslie Howard would play Lawrence. Howard was the actor most often associated with the role and gave a detailed interview to *Film Weekly* in November 1937 outlining how he would play the role (see p. 19). William K. Howard, who had just directed *Fire Over England*, was named as director and it was said that a second unit was leaving for Egypt to shoot location scenes.[19] Continuing problems in Palestine had clearly made a change of location expedient. But now another problem arose which was to sink the project. In order to clear with the Turks the depiction of their part in the story, London Films sent a copy of the script to the Turkish Embassy, asking if there were any alterations they would like to see made. This was standard practice for film companies in the 1930s when scripts featured the activities of 'friendly foreign countries'. On 25 October

Mr Ors, counsellor at the Turkish Embassy, called on G. W. Rendel at the Foreign Office to protest. He told Rendel that in the film 'the Turks were represented as tyrants and oppressors of Arabs, and he felt it was most undesirable that a film which cast such aspersions on Turkish history and national character should be exhibited.' He urged the Foreign Office to discourage its production or at least prevent its being produced in its present form, although he admitted that he could suggest no alterations that would suffice to make it acceptable in Turkish eyes. The Foreign Office was in something of a quandary, being unable to make out whether this London Films production was the same as the New World one or a different project altogether.[20] Rendel recorded his perplexity frankly:

> It is difficult to know what to do about this. When the question originally arose in July 1935, we looked at it mainly from the Arabian angle, since the question at issue was whether there would be any trouble with the Arabs over the shooting of the film so close to Saudi Arabia. It is true that I did allude to the possibility of the Turks resenting any scenes depicting Turkish cruelty, and I believe I even mentioned this to Lt. Colonel Stirling, but I fear we never went into the general question of whether the existence of the film itself would annoy the Turks ... I don't know whether it will be possible to make this film while showing the Turks in a wholly desirable light, but I am afraid that if they were not so represented we are likely to have trouble with them. It is a ridiculous situation when no historical scene can be publicly portrayed for fear of offending those who were once vanquished, and my instinct is not to treat the Turks too tenderly about this. But I suppose that in present international conditions we cannot afford to quarrel with any potential friends, and we must therefore do our best.

He suggested consulting Sir Edward Villiers of New World Films about the problem.[21] By 1 December, they had learned from Sir Edward that he was no longer directly connected with *Revolt in the Desert*, which had reverted to Korda, but was still working with Korda at Denham and would approach him on their behalf.[22] He also made a private suggestion that Korda might be influenced by the use of the honours list. H. L. Baggallay reported on 3 December under the heading 'Most Confidential' that Sir Edward felt sure that 'Mr K., in spite of his protestations about such things, looked forward to a knighthood, possibly in the forthcoming New Year list. If it could be made clear that no knighthood would be forthcoming unless it were understood that the film would be certainly so adapted.' Baggallay said he had no idea whether Korda was in the running for an honour, but it might be checked with the Prime Minister's Office. The suggestion, however, was scotched by Sir Robert Vansittart, the permanent under-secretary, who noted curtly: 'I deprecate any idea of buying him off with a knighthood – if this were done, he need only threaten to produce embarrassing pictures to obtain, eventually, a dukedom!'[23]

More constructively, perhaps, Sir Lancelot Oliphant, the deputy under-secretary for foreign affairs, suggested warning Lord Tyrrell, the president of the British Board of Film Censors (BBFC), of Turkish feelings in this matter and the assistant press officer, Roland Kenney, advised that the Colonial Office get a written undertaking that the finished film would be shown to both the Foreign Office and the Colonial Office before agreeing to grant any further facilities to the company.[24]

Sir Lancelot himself wrote to Lord Tyrrell on 14 December, setting out the whole story, and concluding:

As you know, the Turks are extremely, and to the western mind, rather absurdly sensitive in these matters, but their government is exceedingly friendly and we are anxious to avoid offending them. This consideration leads me to ask whether it lies in your power to do anything to help us, e.g. by stipulating that representatives of the Colonial Office and the Foreign

Office should be offered the opportunity of seeing the film if it is submitted to the British Board of Film Censors. We shall be very grateful for any help you may be able to give us.[25]

Meanwhile, the production of the film was put off yet again and Villiers never did speak to Korda about it. In 1938, Zoltan Korda headed a film unit which went to Egypt and the Sudan to shoot location sequences for *The Four Feathers*, starring John Clements. Sir John Clements later recalled that while they were there, Alexander Korda sent a cable telling them to stay on and shoot exteriors for *Lawrence of Arabia*. But when shooting for *The Four Feathers* ended, the unit returned to Britain and nothing more was said of the Lawrence film until one day Clements asked Korda what had happened and why it had not been made. 'How can I make a film of *Lawrence of Arabia*? We are friendly with the Turks,' replied Korda.[26]

It is clear from this that Alexander Korda ultimately accepted the political situation. But whether it was this or his usual pressing financial problems that caused him once again to dispose of the rights is not clear. For whatever reason, as his subsequent correspondence with the Foreign Office makes clear, he sold the project as a package to Paramount Film Services, the British subsidiary of the Hollywood giant, Paramount Pictures, in 1938. Hollywood had shown considerable interest in the subject of Lawrence of Arabia and both Metro-Goldwyn-Mayer and Universal had registered the title *Lawrence of Arabia* in 1937.[27] But Paramount now apparently stole a march on them by acquiring an already well-developed project.

The delays in filming, which had now gone on for three years, aroused the interest of the press. The *Daily Express* reported on 9 July 1938 that:

the British Foreign Office, acting on representations from the Turkish Government, had intervened to hold up Mr Alexander Korda's plan for a film based on *Revolt in the Desert* by

Lawrence of Arabia. Objection was taken, it was said, to the portrayal of the Turks' wartime defeat by Arabs. Mr Korda said last night: 'I am aware of the Turkish Government's attitude but I have not been approached by the Foreign Office. I anticipate that the film will be produced this autumn.'[28]

As it happened, Sir Robert Vansittart had just signed a contract with Korda to write film scripts on imperial subjects and he was asked to use his influence with the producer of the Lawrence film. Sir Lancelot Oliphant reminded him: 'You of course realize even better than me how much we wish and need to keep the Turks sweet.'[29]

Vansittart duly approached Korda informally and on 25 August 1938 Korda replied to him comprehensively:

I have been very carefully thinking over our conversation about the delicate position in regard to the film *Lawrence of Arabia*. I want to assure you that I would be only too happy to do anything in my power to stop the production of a picture which for some reason or other would be detrimental to national interests. However, after due consideration of all the arguments, I am unable to see how a picture dealing with Lawrence of Arabia could be embarrassing to anybody, and I am, moreover, unable to see my way to advise my company to abandon the production of this picture in view of all the time, trouble and money which have already been expended on the preparations.

He listed his reasons:

1. It is not my company, London Film Productions, which will produce this picture but a wholly-owned subsidiary of an American company to which we have sold our rights and with which company we are only cooperating in an advisory capacity and by selling them our services and studio space for the production of the picture.
2. Since the war, scores of war pictures have been produced showing the German or Austrian officers etc in a somewhat

unfavourable light. I am also quite sure that an equal number of pictures have been produced in Austria and Germany showing officers and soldiers of the French, British or Italian armies in an equally unfavourable light. Still, I have never heard that one of these pictures has been banned on the same grounds for which the Turkish Government now objects to the production of a picture dealing with the life of the late Colonel Lawrence.

3. If the principle on which we are asked to withdraw the production of this picture is accepted, the film industry will be faced with the complete extinction of all historical films, for no picture dealing with either ancient or recent history could be made without showing up some country or other in a light which may be regarded as unfavourable or unpleasant by that country.

4. Even if we were to abandon the making of this picture, it is absolutely certain that some other film company either in England or in America will at some time or other make a film dealing with this subject. I hope you will not interpret it as immodest when I say that if we have a controlling or advisory influence over the actual makers of this picture, there is a much better chance of the film being produced in such a manner as to cause no offence to the Turkish government.

5. I would like to call your attention to the fact that, after all, this picture plays in the time of the old Turkish government, years before the national regeneration of Turkey.

I do not think it is reasonable to demand the full abandonment of this picture. Quite apart from the points mentioned above, we have up till now spent £25,000 on the preparation of this film and in acquiring the film rights of about a dozen books dealing with Lawrence's life.

I am, however, perfectly willing to exercise a restraining influence over the production of the film, and I assure you that the Turkish troops will not be shown in an unfavourable light and that we will not depict any atrocities on their part and generally speaking, short of falsifying history, we will do everything in our power to ensure that this picture will not offend the national sensitivity of the Turkish people.

I am also willing to preface this picture with a foreword (which will be shown wherever the picture is screened) to the effect that the action of the film takes place during the Great War under the old Turkish regime, which was subsequently changed by Kemal Ataturk into the modern Turkey of today, and we will stress the difference between the two forms of government. I should be happy to accept suggestions as to how this foreword should be worded, and frankly speaking, I think that this foreword and the picture following would be rather good propaganda for the enormous change which has taken place in Turkey during the last few years.

I would also be willing to discuss the final scenario either with yourself or someone from the Foreign Office nominated by you in order to try and eliminate anything which in the opinions of that gentleman, might cause unnecessary embarrassment or friction.

Briefly, I am willing to listen to any advice whereby we may safeguard against embarrassment on the part of our own officials and those of the Turkish Government, but I do not consider that it is reasonable to expect us to abandon the project of making a film dealing with such a great national hero as Lawrence of Arabia.[30]

This reply, which shows Korda to be balancing commercial and diplomatic considerations with great delicacy, mollified the Foreign Office, which accepted Korda's offers regarding script and foreword:

Mr Korda's letter is both reasonable and handsome, and I think there is great force in all his points. Indeed, they are unanswerable. The Turks had better accept this favourable attitude – which really amounts to 'arranging' history in their favour, for they committed terrible atrocities – and stop being silly. As Mr Korda says, this doesn't affect modern Turkey at all. I don't believe that in this form Anglo-Turkish relations can be affected in the slightest degree, for they are conditioned by something that is important. And anyhow – since the film will be done by someone – I'd sooner keep Mr Korda's restraining hand on the brake than let it pass entirely into the hands of an American-owned company in England.[31]

However, this apparent harmony between film company and Foreign Office did not last long. On 17 October 1938, Paramount Film Services submitted the script of their proposed film *Lawrence of Arabia* to the British Board of Film Censors. It was read by the chief script-reader, Colonel Hanna, who reported: 'it may not be prohibitive to exhibit a film of this nature at this time but I venture to say emphatically that it would be most impolitic.'[32] He was mainly concerned about upsetting the Arabs and suggested that the Colonial Office should be consulted. But J. Brooke Wilkinson, the BBFC secretary, noted:

> Discussed scenario with Colonel Hanna. I drew his attention to the additional objection the film might have in the Turks, especially in view of a letter addressed some time ago to Lord Tyrrell in the matter from the Foreign Office.[33]

This was Sir Lancelot Oliphant's letter of 14 December 1937 and having been reminded of it, Lord Tyrrell forwarded the script to the Foreign Office.

R. V. Bowker reported that:

> in view of the nature of the passages referring to the Turks, he is doubtful whether the film is altogether suitable for release at the present moment, when the President of Turkey is dangerously ill. He has asked that we would let him know our views, but he has stressed the point that his action is entirely unofficial and that there can be no question of his receiving instructions from the Foreign Office.[34]

Bowker read the script and endorsed Lord Tyrrell's misgivings.

> It is true that the episode of history with which the film deals

was a defeat for the Turks, but it seems hardly necessary, for that reason, that the Turks should invariably be painted – as is the case – in the blackest colours and shown in the most disparaging and humiliating light.[35]

He listed the passages which struck him as the most objectionable, including horrific sequences of massacres perpetrated by the Turks, references to Turkish brutality and torture, and scenes of Turkish callousness and cowardice. Bowker concluded:

> Whether this film is produced now or later there is no doubt that such passages as the foregoing would give offence to the Turks, and I do not think that they would be unduly silly or sensitive in feeling annoyed. I submit that, in replying to Lord Tyrrell, we should call attention to these passages and express our hope that the film will not be released until they have either been cut or drastically revised. We could also let Lord Tyrrell know of Mr Korda's assurances to Sir R. Vansittart … and say that the time seems to have come for him to put into effect his offer to discuss the scenario with us.[36]

Rex Leeper, counsellor at the Foreign Office, wrote to Lord Tyrrell in the terms suggested by Bowker on 2 November 1938, listing the cuts and amendments that would be needed if the script were to be acceptable to the Turks.[37] Lord Tyrrell subsequently telephoned Leeper to say that he had acted in accordance with the Foreign Office suggestions. The action he took is recorded in the BBFC Scenario Reports, where Brooke Wilkinson noted that on 3 November there had been detailed discussions between Lord Tyrrell and his officials and 'eventually it was decided that it would be advisable not to hold out any hope to the producers that the film, if produced, would be certificated'.[38] The company was informed and production was abandoned. Korda reacquired the project rights and in late 1938 there were negotiations with Columbia Pictures for a production starring Cary Grant as Lawrence. But Columbia backed off because of Korda's shaky financial position.[39]

There was, however, to be one final attempt to get *Lawrence of Arabia* off the ground. In May 1939 Korda contacted the Foreign Office to ask if their previous position on the film remained unchanged. He stressed his desire to enlist their help in preparing the final draft of the screenplay and in composing a foreword. J. R. Colville of the Eastern Department minuted the Foreign Office's view:

> As there is no question of meeting the wishes of the Turkish Government to the extent of having the film suppressed altogether, it is important that we should do everything in our power to make it as anodyne as possible, and I think we should certainly not refuse the opportunity now offered us of helping to compose the foreword and of giving our views on the scenario.[40]

C. W. Baxter, acting counsellor at the Foreign Office, wrote to Korda in these terms on 2 June 1939, asking him to send a copy of the script so that the Foreign Office could assess the extent to which it was likely to give offence to the Turks.[41]

Once again there seems to have been verbal contact between Korda and Sir Robert Vansittart on the subject, for Korda wrote to Vansittart on 26 June confirming his willingness 'to collaborate with the Foreign Office in making this picture in such a manner that the Turkish susceptibilities should not be offended'. Korda went on:

> Since our last conversation, I have had the opportunity once more to discuss the problem of the making of this picture with my associates and to emphasize the points which you so kindly raised in various discussions. If I may take your time, I should like to tell you in a few words what sort of picture we want to make of *Lawrence of Arabia*, and I should be exceedingly grateful if you, or some of the experts in the Foreign Office would give an official opinion, as naturally we want to avoid any risk of conflict after the picture is made and after a vast

sum of money has been expended in the making of the film.

My associates and myself are fully convinced that the making of a picture about Lawrence's life is today very greatly in the National Interest, as nothing could have such good propaganda effect as the example of his life.

This company is appreciative of the delicacy of the Turkish problem, and has therefore decided that the picture it is going to make about Lawrence will be based on the following lines:

– about 5 per cent of the picture will be played at Oxford showing Lawrence's life there and his departure for Arabia;

– the second part of the picture, consisting of roughly 45 per cent of the whole film, will be the War Period, in which we will take great care to show the Turks as heroic opponents and to avoid any scenes which would be detrimental to the Turkish people.

I hope that the rest of the picture will present no difficulties at all, as we will deal in passing with Lawrence's work in connection with the Versailles Peace Treaty. We will then carry on to the period of Lawrence's life showing the beginning of the Royal Air Force.

This is by far the most important part of the picture we are planning, and we hope that by showing this unique climax to his life we will make the film more complete and more interesting than if we only concentrated on his exploits in Arabia during the war. By dealing so shortly with the Arabian chapter of Lawrence's life, I feel that our problems regarding any doubts of the Foreign Office will be dealt with much more easily.[42]

Vansittart welcomed the shift of emphasis in the story and wrote back:

The new arrangement of the film ... is, from our point of view, most satisfactory, and we are particularly glad to note that the emphasis of this story is to be shifted from Lawrence's exploits in Arabia to his subsequent career in the Royal Air Force. It seems unlikely that the film, as you describe it, will contain anything at which the Turks can take offence.[43]

Nothing further was heard of the film. It may be that the outbreak of the Second World War and Korda's departure to Hollywood scotched the project finally. But it is clear that it had already moved a long way from the epic retelling of *Revolt in the Desert* originally envisaged. Although the Foreign Office was clearly reluctant to ban the project outright, it was prepared to embark upon a campaign of attrition against it, which involved the use of the BBFC and of informal contacts by Vansittart to influence Korda. It seems unlikely that there would ever have been a script which would have satisfied the Foreign Office and met the objections of the Turks, given the inevitability of depicting the Arab campaign in one form or another.

Korda's rights in *Revolt in the Desert* expired in 1945 and the Lawrence project passed to other hands. There was a major attempt to film Lawrence's life in the mid-1950s, when Terence Rattigan wrote a script which was to be produced for Rank by Anatole de Grunwald and directed by Anthony Asquith with Dirk Bogarde as Lawrence.[44] But just before the film was to begin shooting in 1958, Rank, alarmed at the size of the budget, cancelled it. Rattigan turned his screenplay into a stageplay, *Ross*. Herbert Wilcox, who had rejected the Lawrence project in 1926, purchased the screen rights to *Ross* but was unable to raise finance for filming. Laurence Harvey was front-runner for the role in the project. It was not until 1962 that Lawrence finally reached the screen in David Lean's magisterial epic *Lawrence of Arabia*, starring Peter O'Toole. But Lean's Lawrence was a very different kind of hero from the one envisaged by Korda.

Notes

1. Lowell Thomas, *With Lawrence in Arabia*, London, n.d., p. 11.

2. Herbert Wilcox, *Twenty Five Thousand Sunsets*, London, 1967, p. 204.

3. T. E. Shaw to Rex Ingram, 21 July 1927; Liam O'Leary, *Rex Ingram – Master of the Silent Cinema*, Dublin, 1980, p. x; Adrian Turner, *The Making of David Lean's Lawrence of Arabia*, Limpsfield and London, 1994, p. 26.

4. Robert Morris and Lawrence Raskin, *Lawrence of Arabia: The 30th Anniversary Pictorial History*, New York and London, 1992, p. 15.

5. *Kinematograph Weekly*, 24 May 1934.

6. Jeremy Wilson, *Lawrence of Arabia*, London, 1990, p. 921.

7. P.R.O., FO 371 18925 E 4430/3180/65. Interview between K. W. Blaxter and Lt.-Col. Stirling, 17 July 1935, paragraph 3. Cf. Karol Kulik, *Alexander Korda*, London 1975, pp. 189–90.

8. For a discussion of the film in the context of British film censorship see Jeffrey Richards and Jeffrey Hulbert, 'Censorship in Action: The Case of *Lawrence of Arabia*', *Journal of Contemporary History* 19 (1984), pp. 153–70.

9. Ibid., interview between K. W. Blaxter and Lt.-Col. W. F. Stirling.

10. Ibid., interview between G. W. Rendel and Col. W. F. Stirling, minute 19 July 1935; FO 371 18925 E 5272/3180/65, minute by J. G. Ward, 4 September 1935.

11. FO 371 18925 E 5272/3180/65. Correspondence between O. G. R. Williams, assistant secretary, Colonial Office, and J. Hathorn Hall, chief secretary of the government of Palestine, 13 August and 17 August 1935; departmental memorandum from H. L. Baggallay.

12. *Kinematograph Weekly*, 9 January 1936.

13. Raymond Massey, *A Hundred Different Lives*, London, 1979, p. 62.

14. Kulik, *Alexander Korda*, p. 190.

15. Ibid.

16. *World Film News* 2 (3) (June 1937), p. 10. New World was one of several companies using Denham Studios. In 1937 they produced and released through 20th Century Fox the first British feature film in Technicolor, *Wings of the Morning*, as well as *Under the Red Robe* with Conrad Veidt, *Dinner at the Ritz* with David Niven and *The Green Cockatoo* with John Mills. Both *Wings* and *Dinner at the Ritz* were directed by Harold Schuster. After this, the company ceased to function, victim no doubt of the collapse of the cinema boom that occurred in 1937. The intention was to film *Lawrence* in Technicolor (*Hollywood Reporter*, 27 April 1936).

17. FO 371 20868 E 1745/1745/65, telegram 79064/37 from the colonial secretary to the officer administering the government of

Palestine, 4 March 1937, and reply from that officer to the colonial secretary, 8 March 1937. Cf. letter from K. W. Blaxter to Sir Edward Villiers, 10 March 1937.

18. FO 371 21839 E 7085/1745/65, minutes, 29 November 1937, paragraph 5.

19. *World Film News* 2 (7) (October 1937), p. 18.

20. FO 371 20839 E 6292/65, minutes dated 25 October 1937; comments by J. R. Colville, 26 October 1937.

21. Ibid., comments by G. W. Rendel, 4 November 1937.

22. FO 371 20868 E 7085/1745/65, 1 December 1937, note by Roland Kenney, 21 December 1937.

23. Ibid., note by H. L. Baggallay, 3 December 1937, comment by Sir Robert Vansittart. (Korda was in fact knighted in 1942.)

24. Ibid., comment by Sir Lancelot Oliphant note by Roland Kenney, 21 December 1937.

25. Ibid., letter from Sir Lancelot Oliphant to Lord Tyrrell, 14 December 1937.

26. Kulik, *Alexander Korda*, pp. 190–91.

27. *World Film News* 2 (3) (June 1937), p. 11.

28. *Daily Express*, 9 July 1938.

29. FO 371 21839 E 4804/4356/65. Rundown of situation by H. L. Baggallay, 15 August 1938; letter from Sir Lancelot Oliphant to Sir Robert Vansittart.

30. FO 371 21839 E 5100/4356/65. Letter from Alexander Korda to Sir Robert Vansittart, 25 August 1938, and Vansittart's reply, 31 August 1938.

31. Ibid., comments on the exchange of letters.

32. BBFC *Scenario Reports* 1938, no. 76. Colonel Hanna made a list of scenes that would need deletion if the script were to be passed. They include floggings, hangings, bayonettings, corpses being stripped, brutal battle scenes. But the reasons for the deletions would be that these scenes were regarded as too violent and horrific rather than that they were politically unacceptable.

33. Ibid.

34. FO 371 21839 E 6428/4356/65. Comments from R. V. Bowker, 25 October 1938.

35. Ibid.

36. Ibid.

37. Ibid., letter from R. A. Leeper to Lord Tyrrell, 2 November 1938. It is clear that the deletion suggestions were made by the Foreign Office without reference to the Turkish Embassy.

38. Ibid., comments by R. A. Leeper, H. L. Baggallay, J. R.Colville, R. V. Bowker; BBFC *Scenario Reports* 1938, no. 76.

39. Adrian Turner, *The Making of David Lean's Lawrence of Arabia*, pp. 29–30.

40. FO 371 23194 E 3933/3933/65. J. R. Colville minute, 31 May 1939.

41. Ibid., letter from C. W. Baxter to Alexander Korda, 2 June 1939.

42. FO 371 23194 E 4645/3933/65. Letter from Alexander Korda to Sir Robert Vansittart, 26 June 1939.

43. Ibid., Vansittart's reply.

44. Geoffrey Wansell, *Terence Rattigan*, London 1995, pp. 301–8; Dirk Bogarde, *Snakes and Ladders*, St Albans, 1979, pp. 206–7.

HOW I SHALL PLAY LAWRENCE

Leslie Howard

Leslie Howard gave an interview to J. Danvers Williams in Film Weekly, *20 November 1937, outlining his approach to and plans for the Lawrence film. Reprinted below is the text of the interview.*

'I have played some interesting parts in my time,' said Leslie Howard. 'Somerset Maugham's club-footed introvert in *Of Human Bondage*, the idealistic hero of *The Petrified Forest*, Romeo (such as it was) and, on the stage, Hamlet – but I think the title role in *Lawrence of Arabia* is the greatest acting opportunity of my career.'

I had gone to see Leslie Howard in an effort to clear up the Lawrence mystery. Almost weekly one reads conflicting reports in the newspapers, that the Lawrence film is definitely to be made or that it has been postponed; that a unit is shortly to leave for Arabia, or that the unit has been prevented from starting.

'This film has been in the air so long,' said Howard, 'that it isn't surprising newspapers have become sceptical. The truth is, however, that I am already hard at work on the preliminaries of the picture. Everything is signed and sealed. We hope to start the actual shooting in ten or twelve weeks' time, and have the film edited and ready for presentation by the end of six or eight months.

'I am particularly interested in this picture because I am

co-producing it. Korda is at present busy in America, which means that I shall be virtually in control of the whole production.

'For the first time in my life I shall not be the mere puppet of another man's imagination. I shall be able to place on the screen my own undiluted conception of Lawrence of Arabia, and if the final result does not measure up to expectations I shall, at least, have the satisfaction of knowing that I have only myself to blame.

'At the moment, of course, I think we have a chance of making a first-class picture. Certainly, the story itself has all the aspects of a great drama.

'One of the chief reasons Korda has refrained so long from putting the picture into production is that he found it difficult to produce a scenario, a director and an actor whom he felt would do the subject justice.

'It is not the sort of film that anyone could make. You can rule out most of the ace directors – such as Capra, Lubitsch and Borzage – as types of mentalities who would be quite out of their depth in a picture of this sort. Off-hand, I can think of only two directors whom I would care to employ – John Ford, who made *The Informer*, and William K. Howard, who has actually been given the assignment.

'When the film was first mooted two or three years ago, Korda offered me the chief part, but I declined it as I did not consider any of the directors he then had under contract suitable for the picture. If the film was to be made at all, I felt that it must be made imaginatively by a serious-minded and expert craftsman. The picture must be free altogether of the Bengal Lancer aspect; it must have nothing Kiplingesque or sentimental; above all, it must have no shrieking Arabs riding across the desert in the manner of cowboys.

'Bill Howard is the ideal person for the job. His American films like *Transatlantic* and *Power and the Glory* show that he can penetrate beyond the superficial actions of his characters and show an audience what is going on in their minds. I think that he is capable of capturing the drama and the mysticism of Lawrence's Arabian adventure.

'He and I have been working together on this project for some time. A provisional scenario has been prepared, but as yet neither of us is satisfied. Our intention is to work it all out very carefully beforehand, so that when we arrive in Arabia he will only have to face the purely mechanical problem of photographing the film, and I shall be able to devote all my time to the characterisation.

'I hope to bring in Winston Churchill to complete the scenario. He is one of the few statesmen of the period who saw beyond Lawrence's military importance into the real complexities of his nature.

'Already, in a number of informal conversations, Churchill has helped me considerably to round off my impression of Lawrence. A truly tragic figure, Lawrence is an absorbing character for an actor to recreate. One has only to read *The Seven Pillars of Wisdom* to realise that Lawrence was a poet with great powers of perception; yet although he cultivated many literary men (like Shaw and Thomas Hardy) with whom he came into contact, he was himself too much of an ascetic to commit his more intimate musings to paper.

'His habit of motor-cycling was quite typical of him. He believed that luxury was bad for the soul and found virtue in discomfort.

'Despite the documentary value of *The Seven Pillars of Wisdom* and its penetrating flashes of poetry, it is written in the slightly self-conscious style of an undergraduate. In fact, when Lawrence first began to organise the Arabs he was little more than that – twenty-six to be exact. The influence of Oxford was still upon him. He was naïve, youthful and incredibly idealistic.

'An idealist he remained until his death, despite all that he saw and suffered. When France and Britain decided to divide up the administration of Arabia after the war, Lawrence felt that he had betrayed the trust placed in him by the Arab chieftains – that, all along, he had been merely the tool of a political machine. In order to atone for what he considered a grave political injustice, he retired to a country cottage, refusing the honours which the state wished to bestow upon him, refusing even to be known by his own name.

'It is Lawrence's own personal drama – his enthusiasm, his strength of character, his endurance, his bravery, his fine perception and his moments of fear and resentment – which will form the basis of the picture.

'At the beginning we shall show him sent to Arabia because he happens to have spent a long vacation there and knows the language. His importance as yet unsuspected by the British authorities, he goes off to find an Arab ruler capable of banding together the many tribes and driving the Turks out of Palestine. He meets Abdulla and finds him too clever. Ali is too meticulous and Zied too callous. Then, at last, he meets Feisal, a man of great sagacity and enthusiasm, and in what should be a remarkably powerful sequence realises that this is the person he has been searching for.

'Almost against his will, Lawrence is drawn closely into the campaign. He sees the months of striving and privation which lie before him, yet a man such as he is needed to plan the war, to settle the internal squabbling of the Arab chiefs and to urge them on to victory. So, outwardly, he becomes one of them; wears their clothes and eats their food, is scorched by the midday sun and frozen by the cold winds of the night, until he himself becomes fired with the enterprise. Yet there are moments when he is utterly miserable.

'In *The Seven Pillars of Wisdom* he says: "The effort of these years to live in the dress of the Arabs and to imitate their mental foundation, quitted me of my English self, and let me look at the West and its conventions with new eyes: they destroyed it all for me. At the same time, I could not sincerely take on the Arab skin: it was an affectation only. I had dropped one form and not taken on the other … with a resultant feeling of intense loneliness in life, and a contempt, not for other men, but for all they do. Such detachment came at times to a man exhausted by long physical effort and isolation. His body plodded on mechanically, while his reasonable mind left him, and from without looked down critically on him, wondering what that futile lumber did and why. Sometimes these selves would converse in the void; and then madness was very near, as I believe it would be near any man who could see things through the veils at one of two customs, two educations, two environments."

'But this pathetic, introspective Lawrence was never apparent to his Arab followers. During the day he remained the calm and ruthless man of action. He blew up train-loads of Turks, demolished towns, and on one occasion shot out the brains of a lieutenant because he feared that the man's influence might demoralise the army. Only as he lay alone at night did the memory of the dead return to haunt him.

'All these things must be captured in the picture. I intend to show the working of Lawrence's mind by the simple device of spoken thoughts. The camera will usually show him as the self-possessed leader, but sometimes, when he is quite alone, his innermost thoughts will rise to the surface.

'We shall have to be very careful with these soliloquies – they tend to become bathetic. But I think that, used economically and with great discretion, they should prove very effective and should give the picture just that touch of introspection which will make it something more than a mere adventure story.

'I want to avoid that above all else. I should like the picture, as it progresses, to take on the shape of a tragedy: the ultimate defeat of all Lawrence's ideals by the well-meaning, uncompromising machine of British government.

'There is something essentially tragic about the situation in which Lawrence finds himself. Towards the end of the scenario there is a scene in which he meets the Arab leaders after the British Government has decided (against his advice) to mandate certain portions of Palestine. Lawrence himself is the only person who does not know their decision.

'The chiefs greet him with stony silence. They believe that he has betrayed them in the moment of victory. Resentful and powerless to alter the decision of the government, Lawrence returns home to do his great penance.

'In the final sequence I hope to show him riding to his death along a country lane on his powerful motor cycle. Then some sort of quick shot back to Palestine with its intrigues and insurrections – a tormented stretch of land which, if only Lawrence had had his way, might now have been a peaceful and united country.'

LAWRENCE OF ARABIA: THE SCREENPLAY

Reproduced here is the last version of the screenplay Korda commissioned. It is dated 4 October 1938, though it is little different from the one other surviving screenplay prepared a few months earlier. Although earlier screenplays exist – these are in the library of the British Film Institute, London – there are no surviving versions following this. It represents Korda's final attempt – after many years of work – to film the life of Lawrence.

LAWRENCE OF ARABIA

from

Revolt In The Desert

by T. E. Lawrence

Scenario by Miles Malleson,
Brian Desmond Hurst
and Duncan Guthrie

OCTOBER 4th 1938

After titles we dissolve to (to be shown on the screen): dedication

> I LOVED YOU, SO I DREW THESE TIDES OF MEN
>   INTO MY HANDS
> AND WROTE MY WILL ACROSS THE SKY IN STARS
> TO EARN YOU FREEDOM ...

T. E. Lawrence

1. *Carchemish. As titles fade the screen is held completely dark for a few moments. Loud cracks from a viciously lashing whip are heard. The screen clears to show the face of an* ARAB BOY *in agony. With each lash the muscles of his face tighten. His teeth are clenched, his eyes closed in pain, but he is determined to make no sound. Camera withdraws, showing that he is held tightly against a post and each wrist is grasped by a* SOLDIER *who leans back away from the lash of the whip. The* BOY *is being flogged by a* MAN. *An* ENGINEER *strolls into the picture and motions him to stop. The soldiers release the* BOY. *As he stumbles out of the picture they take a final slash at him.*

SOLDIER: Arab swine.

2. *A hand delicately brushing away fragments of earth from a Hittite slab. Camera withdraws, revealing* LAWRENCE *at work and behind him the excavations. Lines of* ARABS *carry baskets full of earth from where others are digging. They carry them up an incline from the excavation pits and empty them in front of the sorters. As they work they chant over and over again 'Kam loilo. Kam yome.' ('How many nights, how many days until I reach my beloved.') As the camera comes to rest* DAHOUM *enters shot, sits down beside* LAWRENCE *and silently picking up his sieve starts to sift the earth.* LAWRENCE *looks up and sees* DAHOUM'*s back.*

LAWRENCE (*quietly*): Who was it, Dahoum?

DAHOUM *bends over his work and does not answer.* LAW-RENCE *rises and comes to* DAHOUM.

LAWRENCE: Dahoum, who did it to you?

Track closer.

DAHOUM (*reluctantly*): One of the engineers working on the railway.

LAWRENCE *puts down his sieve and walks away without a word. The camera pans, holding* LAWRENCE *as he walks towards the railway. Dissolve.*

3. LAWRENCE *entering the camp, the camera tracking with him as he approaches the* ENGINEER.

LAWRENCE: One of your men assaulted my servant.

ENGINEER: Nonsense! He merely had him flogged.

LAWRENCE: Well, don't you call that an assault?

ENGINEER: Certainly not. You can't use these natives without flogging them. We have men thrashed every day – it's the only way.

LAWRENCE: You won't build your Berlin to Baghdad railway by flogging Arabs. That engineer of yours must come and apologise.

ENGINEER: Nonsense. The incident is closed.

LAWRENCE: On the contrary. If you don't do as I ask I shall take your engineer down to the village and there flog him.

ENGINEER: You couldn't and daren't do such a thing.

LAWRENCE (*ominously*): I could and I dare!

The ENGINEER *sees the determination on* LAWRENCE*'s face. Camera centres on the engineer, as* LAWRENCE *walks out of the picture.*

ENGINEER (*mutters*): Very well!

4. *The excavations. For a few moments the working and singing continues. Then, suddenly, one of the Arabs leaps out of the pit and fires his gun into the air, the signal for an important find. All the Arabs seem to go mad, dance, shout and shriek. There is indescribable pandemonium. They rush towards him.* THE SAME. *The Arab leaps into the pit and starts scrabbling the earth.* THE SAME. THE SAME. *Lawrence runs into the excited, shouting group.* LAWRENCE, *the* ARAB *and the statue. They work away at clearing the statue. As they dig the earth from it, a pair of very English legs come into shot behind* LAWRENCE.

ENGLISHMAN'S VOICE: Hullo T.E.! Have you heard the news? There's trouble in the Balkans.

Lawrence does not look round.

LAWRENCE (*offhandedly*): There's always trouble in the Balkans. (*Speaking proudly*): Look at this Hittite statue. Isn't it a beauty?

The ENGLISHMAN *kneels down beside him.*

ENGLISHMAN: I'm afraid it'll mean war.

The camera tracks up to LAWRENCE *as he speaks.*

LAWRENCE: Well, if there is a war it won't touch us.

Dissolve to:

5. *Close shot (same size shot as above). The Arab Intelligence Department, Cairo.* LAWRENCE *is turning over papers on his desk. We see*

that now he is dressed in officer's uniform. The camera tracks back and we see another SUBALTERN — *the same Englishman who was with* LAWRENCE *at Carchemish — and at a telegraphic receiving apparatus a* VERY YOUNG SUBALTERN. *As the camera tracks* LAWRENCE *turns and speaks to the* SUBALTERN.

LAWRENCE: We're in it all right — up to the neck. Held up in France ... Kitchener dead ... The Dardanelles evacuated ... Kut captured by the Turks, and now they're threatening Suez.

SUBALTERN: No wonder we're getting the wind up. I counted sixty-five generals going into the conference this morning.

LAWRENCE: There were only sixty-four. You must have counted the fat one twice.

The VERY YOUNG SUBALTERN *comes up to them with a message in his hand.*

VERY YOUNG SUBALTERN: I say, Bill, for the Lord's sake, help me out. I can't make head or tail of this Arab stuff.

SUBALTERN: Ask T.E. He knows more about Arabs than I do.

LAWRENCE: Let's have a look.

LAWRENCE takes the message and reads it. As he reads the COLONEL comes in and they stand to attention.

LAWRENCE: What's that?

The COLONEL *takes the message and reads it:*

COLONEL: Our agent in Damascus says the Turks are only waiting for an opportunity to arrest Feisal. Absolute nonsense! The Turks would never do that.

LAWRENCE (*abruptly*): It's the next thing they *will* do.

Cut to: close shot. The COLONEL *angrily glares at* LAWRENCE.

He looks down at his feet. Cut to: close up. LAWRENCE's *feet. He is wearing dancing pumps. Cut to: medium shot. The* COLONEL *and* LAWRENCE. *The* COLONEL *is furious.*

COLONEL: Do you usually wear pumps in the office?

LAWRENCE: Yes, sir.

COLONEL: Why?

LAWRENCE: More comfortable, sir.

COLONEL: And what do you suppose would happen if we all wore what we liked?

LAWRENCE: We should all be more comfortable, sir.

The VERY YOUNG SUBALTERN *laughs. The* COLONEL *turns towards the* VERY YOUNG SUBALTERN, *who quickly pretends to be very intent on his work. The* COLONEL *turns back to* LAWRENCE.

COLONEL: I'm sorry to interfere in any way with your comfort, but *I'm afraid* I must insist on boots.

Close shot. The COLONEL. *He speaks with heavy sarcasm.*

COLONEL: I hope you don't mind.

Cut to: medium shot. LAWRENCE.

LAWRENCE: No Sir – Anything to help win the war.

LAWRENCE *slips back into his seat and the camera tracks close up to his hands, which take an unfinished sketch map of Arabia. He picks up a pencil and writes, in the correct place, the word Damascus. Dissolve to:*

6. *Extreme long shot. Dawn. Damascus. Quiet, peaceful voice of* MUEZZIN *heard softly intoning the call to prayer.*

7. *Closer shot. The* MUEZZIN. *During the mix* MUEZZIN's *voice becomes louder.*

MUEZZIN'S VOICE: God alone is great: I testify there are no Gods but God: and Mohammed is his prophet. Come to prayer, come to security ...

Abrupt cut to:

8. *Rows of feet standing on barrels. The composition of the shot is so arranged that we cannot see more than the lower part of the bodies. We see by their robes they are* ARABS. SOLDIERS *pass across the scene kicking away the barrels as they go. The bodies remain suspended in the air, their legs kicking convulsively. These scenes are dimly observed on background of action and are obscured by smoke from sentries' fires. The camera tracks back disclosing* JEMAL PASHA *and an* OFFICER *watching indifferently. They move along the line of bodies and the camera tracks ahead of them. They meet, and the camera comes to rest on a tall* ARAB, *in Turkish uniform, except for Arab headdress, who watches the executions. Beyond him is a great iron cage, packed with Arab prisoners. The* OFFICER *speaks with ironical politeness.*

OFFICER: Ah, Prince Feisal, you have come out to see the sights?

FEISAL *gives a fleeting glance at the bodies. The Turkish* OFFICER *catches the glance.*

OFFICER: Regrettable, but quite unavoidable. We are at war.

JEMAL PASHA: And we need hardly point out to a man of your knowledge and discretion –

JEMAL PASHA *produces a gold cigarette case.*

... won't you smoke?

FEISAL: Thank you, no.

JEMAL PASHA: That this war will mean the speedy collapse of Great Britain – and with Great Britain the whole British Empire. It will mean freedom for several hundred million of the faithful.

TURKISH OFFICER: To achieve this we must have the loyal support of your people.

FEISAL (*almost in spite of himself*): And you think that (*he indicates the bodies*) is the way to gain their loyalty.

JEMAL PASHA: After all, Prince Feisal, we both have one thing at heart – Victory over the Infidel. There is nothing that need stand between us.

FEISAL (*quietly*): Only thousands of dead Arabs.

JEMAL PASHA (*angrily*): Those are dangerous words, Prince Feisal.

FEISAL *turns and walks away.* JEMAL PASHA *and the* TURKISH OFFICER *watch him with hatred in their faces. Cut to:* JEMAL PASHA *and the* TURKISH OFFICER.

JEMAL PASHA: The only way to get *obedience* from an Arab is to treat him like the slave and dog he is.

OFFICER: And there goes the cleverest and most dangerous of them all.

JEMAL PASHA: He is under our eyes and harmless.

OFFICER: He would be more harmless at the end of a rope.

They smile. Cut to:

9. *Cairo. The passage outside the Arab Intelligence Department's Office. An* ORDERLY *comes along the passage carrying an envelope. He goes through a door marked 'Arab Intelligence Dept.'. Cut to:*

10. *Inside the office. The* ORDERLY *enters, presents the* COL-ONEL *with an official looking envelope and retires. The* COLONEL. *He opens the envelope.*

COLONEL: Nothing of importance. (*He adds, casually – as he crumples the official Report and tosses it into the waste-paper basket*): The Turks in Damascus have strung up another batch of Arabs.

LAWRENCE. *He looks up from his map.*

LAWRENCE (*quietly*): You call that of no importance, Sir?

The COLONEL *and* LAWRENCE.

COLONEL: Except to the poor devils who've been strung up – No!

LAWRENCE (*perfectly politely*): I don't agree.

The two young SUBALTERNS. *An exchange of looks.*

LAWRENCE (*contrite*): I'm sorry, sir. I didn't mean to contradict. (*He adds, quietly*): But as this is the Arab Intelligence Department, I thought a little intelligence about the Arabs mightn't be out of place!

He is intent on his map.

11. *The map itself. It has advanced a little further. And even as we see it, he draws a line East of Gaza and one North of Musul and writes, between the lines, the words 'Under Turkish domination'.*

LAWRENCE'S VOICE: I've been expecting it ... waiting for it ... any day, now –

12. *The* COLONEL *and* LAWRENCE.

COLONEL: What are you talking about?

LAWRENCE: The revolt of the Arabs.

COLONEL: Stuff and nonsense! No organisation!

LAWRENCE: No organisation, sir?! – With their secret societies?

COLONEL: I know all about *them*! *Debating* societies!

LAWRENCE: More than that, sir. There's a complete underground network of them: all over Arabia.

COLONEL: *Talk*! Secret, underground talk, that's all ... Whispering what you have to say doesn't make it more dangerous!

LAWRENCE: I wonder! *Having* to whisper makes you want to shout ... And Arabs of every rank and condition are whispering ... Arabs who are highly placed officers in the Turkish army –

COLONEL: A Revolt! ... No! ... They'd be smashed in a day ... Never get the Arabs to unite. Never. No leader.

LAWRENCE: There's Feisal. He's an Arab prince, son of King of Hussein of Mecca, and an unwilling officer in the Turkish Army.

COLONEL: Not only an officer in the Turkish army – but actually an enforced guest of the Turkish high command at Damascus – *and* a member of one of these revolutionary Arab secret societies.

The COLONEL *turns to* LAWRENCE. *The* COLONEL *and* LAWRENCE.

COLONEL (*to Lawrence with a humour of his own*): Correct me if I'm wrong.

LAWRENCE: Quite right, sir. There's a very powerful one in Damascus and Feisal's the head of it.

Cut to:

13. *Long shot. Bazaar, Damascus.* FEISAL *walking through the crowded bazaar. His eyes downcast. But he is obviously on the outlook. A* LEMONADE SELLER *with all his paraphernalia. They see one another.* FEISAL *stops and buys a drink from the* LEMONADE SELLER. *He pours a drink from his long spouted jar, and, as* FEISAL *pays, we see the* LEMONADE SELLER *slip a note into* FEISAL's *hand.* FEISAL *walks on. The* LEMONADE SELLER *stands watching* FEISAL. *As soon as* FEISAL *has gone – a* TURK *comes casually up to him to buy a drink … But the* LEMONADE SELLER *suddenly finds himself handcuffed. Immediately another* TURK, *who has been waiting ready, comes up. The* LEMONADE SELLER *is led away, handcuffed between the two* TURKS.

14. *Damascus. A meeting of an Arab secret society.* FEISAL *presiding. Several other* ARAB CHIEFS. *Some in Arab dress: others of various ranks in the Turkish army.* FEISAL *unfolds the note given him by the lemonade seller and scans it. The others wait, expectant.*

FEISAL: From my father – all is ready. He says here: that to allay the suspicions of the Turks, he has ordered a review of Arab troops … outside the walls of Medina … But now he can barely restrain them from attacking the town at once … They wait only for us.

ONE OF THE CHIEFS (*amending*): Only for you.

FEISAL (*accepting the amendment*): For me.

FEISAL *sets light to the paper and watches it burn. The others watch* FEISAL.

ONE OF THE CHIEFS: You will go?

FEISAL (*slowly*): Not yet.

ANOTHER OF THE CHIEFS: 'Not yet'! When every day more of our people are butchered: and every day – more ...

FEISAL: It needs more courage to wait than to strike ... yet must we wait ...

An ARAB *bursts into the meeting. Consternation and apprehension. The* NEWCOMER *goes straight to* FEISAL.

THE NEWCOMER: El-Kahn the water seller has been arrested!

FEISAL: When?

THE NEWCOMER: You had scarce gone from him ... The Turks have gone to your house. They will arrest you too.

FEISAL. *He considers this new situation, for a moment, then:*

FEISAL: We meet at the South Gates of the City: just before they close. And ride out ... Tonight.

15. *The gates of Damascus. Night. Just as they are being closed a small group of Arabs – among whom is* FEISAL *– gallops through them – and out into the desert.*

16. *A map, centred on Damascus. The camera pans down the map while doubly printed across it we see the galloping horsemen of* FEISAL's *followers and other tribes who hurry to join him. The camera becomes static again when Medina is in the centre of the screen.*

17. *An Arab encampment. Outside the walls of Medina. A portion of the Arab Army. A fine, tho' mixed-looking lot of men, something of a rabble, and with the most extraordinary assortment of arms – from antiquated old muskets to spears, knives and shields.* FEISAL *appears, on horseback. When the drums begin to beat, the camels are*

loaded hurriedly. *After the second signal everyone leaps into the saddle and draws off to left or right, leaving a broad lane up which* FEISAL *rides on his mare with* SHARRAF *a pace behind him, and then* ALI, *the standard-bearer, a splendid, wild man from Nejd, with his hawk's face framed in long plaits of jet-black hair falling downward from his temples.* ALI *is dressed garishly and rides a tall camel. Behind him are the mob of sherifs, sheikhs and slaves.*

18. *Medina. On the city walls. A group of* TURKISH OFFICERS. *They are looking towards the* ARABS – *through field-glasses. As they sweep the view, with their glasses, we see what they see.*

19. *Sections of the Arab Army as it charges. One notices again the magnificent physique of the men and their extraordinary collection of weapons. Their frenzied on-coming, ever-nearing rush is terrific; awe-inspiring.*

20. *The* TURKISH OFFICERS. *Watching. The* SENIOR OFFICER *taking his field-glasses from his eyes, gives a short sharp command in the direction of* –

21. *A field-gun. The very latest from a western armament factory, a scientific, exquisite, exact, deadly machine of destruction, and manned by a well-trained, automatic, khaki-clad Turkish gun crew. It fires. Another gun; and its crew; every movement similar … it fires. Another … and it fires. Another … and it fires. Another … and it fires.*

22. *Long shot. Arabs in full retreat. Cut to:*

23. *Medium close shot. Ext. Walls of Medina. Ben Ali tribe approach walls of Medina carrying white flag. Cut to:*

24. *Medium close shot. Int. Walls of Medina. Ben Ali tribe carrying white flag, being accorded safe escort into the city. Quick dissolve to:*

25. *Int. Headquarters of Turkish command in Medina.* FAKHRI PASHA *– Turkish Commander – flanked by staff officers receives the delinquent tribesmen.*

BEN ALI SHEIKH: We offer submission.

FAKHRI: On what terms?

BEN ALI SHEIKH: That our village be spared.

FAKHRI: What is the name of your village?

BEN ALI SHEIKH: Awali.

FAKHRI (*dismissing the tribesmen with a wave of his hand*): Your village will be spared.

As the TRIBESMEN *retire from the room* FAKHRI *turns to a Turkish* CAVALRY OFFICER.

FAKHRI: Shukri Bey!

TURKISH LANCER (*stepping forward*): Yes, sir.

FAKHRI (*smiling*): You have your orders.

26. *Back in Cairo. A corner of the* COLONEL*'s private room, in the 'Arab Intelligence Department'. The* COLONEL *has a friend of his, a* STAFF CAPTAIN, *with him. And the* COLONEL *is very cock-a-hoop.* LAWRENCE *is just entering the room.*

COLONEL: Well, young man! What did I tell you! ... 'Smashed in a day.'

LAWRENCE: Yes, sir.

STAFF CAPTAIN: In a few minutes apparently! A couple of

whizz-bangs, and the Arabs were doing a marathon into the desert.

LAWRENCE: A great disappointment.

COLONEL: Foregone conclusion!

STAFF CAPTAIN: What else did you expect! An isolated, local rising!

LAWRENCE: That's true, sir! ... out of sheer desperation ... Despair can inspire courage: but it wants a deeper inspiration.

The COLONEL's *look at* LAWRENCE *is half-amused, half-pitying. We should feel that although* LAWRENCE *exasperates him, he can't help liking him; recognising him as out of the common.*

COLONEL: 'Inspiration'? ... For what?

LAWRENCE: For a united effort to throw off the Turkish yoke; once and for all; to gain their freedom.

LAWRENCE: Men always fight the better in a great cause. Give the Arab a leader, someone whom they follow in a fight for their own independence; even to recreate their Empire –

STAFF CAPTAIN: The Babylonians had an Empire! And the Hittites – or whatever you call 'em – and where are they now? Dust!

COLONEL: Young man, you've a bee in your bonnet! And that reminds me, that cap you go about in is a disgrace! Go to the stores and get a new one ...

LAWRENCE: Yes, sir.

STAFF CAPTAIN: The Arab of today isn't what he *was*! ... You never know where you *are* with him –

LAWRENCE (*starting to speak*): Yes, sir – but –

COLONEL: I know what you're going to say!! 'You don't agree'!!

LAWRENCE (*with a wry smile*): How can I, sir? ... I happen to have travelled a good many thousand miles among them, alone. I know something of them – at least enough to know that they're really no different from us!

STAFF CAPTAIN: No different!!

LAWRENCE: No, sir. Just as reasonable. Just as good, and just as bad ... After all, they live in a land that cradled the three great religions of the world – Jewry, Christianity and Islam. And they have the capacity for following a great ideal to the death, or to its attainment.

COLONEL: Sounds very fine, but it's bosh for all that! A queer customer – your Arab! ... Inscrutable ... Hasn't got our standards! You can't trust him, any more than you can understand him ...

LAWRENCE (*suddenly angry*): There's nothing *inscrutable* about the Arabs ... the word's an excuse for not *troubling* to know them ... It's just *laziness* to say they can't be understood, and *prejudice* to say they can't be trusted!

COLONEL (*very angry too*): Laziness and prejudice! ... Lawrence!

LAWRENCE: Sir?

COLONEL: When you get that new cap, you can take ten days' leave in it and when you come back, I'll have found another job for you – where your crack-brained ideas about the Arabs won't be such a handicap to you!!!

27. *Ext. Valley of Wadi Safre. Day. The hidden valley is occupied by*

FEISAL's *defeated army. They sprawl about like lazy scorpions beneath every great rock, bush and clump of trees, exposing their brown limbs to the shade. The saddle camels are grazing on the slopes.*

28. FEISAL. *He is standing, framed between the black uprights of a doorway; very tall and pillarlike, very slender in his long white silk robes and his brown head-cloth bound with scarlet and gold cord. He stands in an attitude of waiting, his eyes gazing toward the opening of the valley. Suddenly his attention is drawn to a strange figure in the distance.*

29. *From* FEISAL's *angle. Appearing over a distant ridge and riding down the valley on a camel, comes a strange figure wearing English field uniform and Arabian headdress. He is escorted by two Arabs. They ride up to* FEISAL's *house. A guide speaks to the sentries. They enter.* LAWRENCE *dismounts and goes directly to* FEISAL. *For a moment the two stand looking at one another — both seem to realise that this is an historic, a fateful encounter.*

LAWRENCE: Prince Feisal?

FEISAL *acknowledges the greeting with a bow.*

FEISAL: El Lurens?

LAWRENCE *bows as* FEISAL *turns and makes way for him.*

30. *Int.* FEISAL's *room at Hamra. The semi-darkness of the room hides many silent figures who gaze steadily at* LAWRENCE. FEISAL *is sitting on his carpet facing the door. He stares down at his hands, which are twisting slowly about his dagger.*

FEISAL (*softly*): How did you find the journey?

LAWRENCE: The heat was oppressive.

FEISAL: And how do you like our place here at Wadi Safra?

LAWRENCE (*after a significant pause*): Well, but it is far from Damascus.

The word falls like a sword in their midst. There is a quiver – everyone present seems to hold his breath.

FEISAL (*looking directly into Lawrence's eyes*): Praise be to God there are Turks nearer to us than that.

LAWRENCE.

LAWRENCE (*reminding him softly of the defeat at Medina*): Yes, and Turkish artillery too!

FEISAL.

FEISAL (*suddenly brought back to earth*): My men are not afraid of bullets or death.

Feisal's voice is soft and even, though he is obviously controlling it with an effort.

FEISAL: But modern artillery they had never known before. And when the Turkish shells fell among them, they broke ... Then the Beni-Ali tribe surrendered: and laid down their arms, on condition their village was not destroyed ... And the Turks took their arms – and destroyed their village ... Not a man, woman or child was spared ... Living and dead alike were thrown into the flames.

A terrible little wave of sound sweeps round the semi-circle. Close-ups of two or three of the CHIEFS *– Horror: helpless rage: despair in their faces. They mutter short phrases in Arabic – little moans and cries.*

FEISAL.

FEISAL: There is more – but I cannot speak of it ... the Turk knows well the art of killing – of killing fast and killing slow ... And the story of this infamy has spread across the desert and sent a shock across all Arabia ... So now there can be no question of submission. Yet victory seems impossible.

LAWRENCE. *He uses, curiously but naturally, the same tones and inflections as Feisal.*

LAWRENCE: Yet, by this very act, the Turks may have sealed their own doom, not yours.

Now every pair of Arab eyes looks towards LAWRENCE. *And wide-open, in growing amazement.*

FEISAL: How so?

LAWRENCE: I know it is not possible for you to fight as they fight, for the first rule in *your* warfare is that women are inviolable: the second, that the lives of children too young to fight with men must be spared: and the third, that property impossible to carry off, shall be left undamaged.

FEISAL: You know much of the Arabs.

LAWRENCE: It is because I know and love your people – that I, a stranger, have dared to come to you here.

More and more, as he gets into the atmosphere, LAWRENCE – *'The Chameleon of a man' – is using their cadences and idiom. And he does this half unconsciously and altogether without effort.*

LAWRENCE: You say defeat is inevitable. Yet you have but one victory to gain – over yourselves.

Close shots of the CHIEFS. *It is as if all eyes were held to him by a tight cord. And more and more his quiet voice seems to fill the tent.*

LAWRENCE'S VOICE: You are a divided people: your ancient blood feuds keep tribe against tribe; each chief is for himself; often his greatest enemy is his nearest neighbour.

LAWRENCE: You say that the massacre of the Beni Ali is known all over Arabia ... Then let the blood that was shed there unite you into a nation. Let the fire that destroyed that village burn out all the jealousies and rivalries from your hearts; and weld you into One. Then there can be no defeat.

FEISAL. *He is deeply moved.*

FEISAL: You speak truths that must find an echo in every Arab heart.

THE CHIEFS. A deep murmur of assent runs round the tent.

LAWRENCE. *As he realises the effect of his words.*

FEISAL: Yet how can even this Truth prevail against Guns?

LAWRENCE: Prince Feisal – and you – (*he turns to the other chiefs and names them easily by name*)

The CHIEFS *are obviously impressed and pleased.*

... you have done me the honour to receive me, and to listen to me –

LAWRENCE *turns direct to* FEISAL.

... if you will undertake to raise an army, and move to capture Wehj – which must be the first step towards Damascus –

Another crescendo, deep murmur shows that they are hanging on every word.

LAWRENCE: – then I – for my part – undertake that you shall be supplied with guns, with arms, with money ...

FEISAL *and* LAWRENCE. FEISAL *looks at* LAWRENCE *in amazement.*

FEISAL: In whose name can you make such a promise?

LAWRENCE.

LAWRENCE: In the name of the British Government!!!

31. *Back in the* COLONEL'*s room, in Cairo. The* COLONEL *and* LAWRENCE ... *This time, the* COLONEL *is really upset.*

COLONEL (*loud, in emphatic exasperation*): Can't you do *anything* like other people? When I give a young man ten days' leave, I expect him to *take* ten days – not five!! Found the time hang heavy, I suppose – *mooning* about, doing nothing ...

LAWRENCE: No, sir.

COLONEL: Oh! ... What have you been doing?

LAWRENCE: I've been on a visit to Prince Feisal.

COLONEL: You've been what?!?

LAWRENCE (*going on, as if he were saying the most ordinary things in the world*): I'd never met him, sir ... I've always thought he might be the Prophet-Leader I was looking for.

COLONEL: Prophet-Leader *you* were looking for!

LAWRENCE: Yes, sir ... and I was right. He is.

COLONEL: Have *you* gone mad, or have I?

LAWRENCE: There's a War on, sir – maybe we're all mad!

COLONEL (*trying to get some sense out of it*): Prophet-Leader indeed! And now you've found him what are you going to *do* with him ...

LAWRENCE: I promised him help!

COLONEL: ... What help?

LAWRENCE: Supplies.

COLONEL (*getting most ominously quieter*): What supplies?

LAWRENCE: Machine-guns. Rifles. Ammunition. Money. *Artillery.*

COLONEL (*now quite quiet, and immensely serious: very much superior officer – and rather terrifying*): So you *mean* all this?

LAWRENCE: Yes, sir.

COLONEL: You will remain here, till I send for you ...

And the COLONEL *turns quickly on his heel and goes straight from the room. Camera tracks close to* LAWRENCE. *Mix:*

32. *Military Headquarters in Cairo.* LAWRENCE. *The camera tracks back from* LAWRENCE *to include the* G.O.C. *(General Officer Commanding).* LAWRENCE *is standing before him. The* G.O.C. *is leaning back in his chair, taking stock of the young man in front of him. There is a tiny silence.*

G.O.C.: And these promises! ... On whose authority did you make them?

LAWRENCE: My own.

G.O.C.: Your rank?

LAWRENCE: Second Lieutenant.

G.O.C.: A little unusual?!

LAWRENCE: The whole situation's unusual.

G.O.C.: How?

LAWRENCE: It wasn't just an idea of the moment, sir. It's been in my mind for months.

G.O.C. (*non-committal*): ... Well?

LAWRENCE: From the view-point of the world war, sir: among our enemies, the Turks are the weakest link – to smash that link would strike a tremendous blow for the Allies.

LAWRENCE *is talking in quite different tones and intonations than he used to the Arabs. His manner maintains a certain diffidence, but at the same time he is unembarrassed by the other's eminence. He is persuasive, reasonable, 'English', man-to-man. The* G.O.C.'s *keen humorous eyes are intent on* LAWRENCE, *and behind those eyes, the fate of the Arab revolt hangs in the balance.*

LAWRENCE – *who knows this.*

LAWRENCE: One can't over-estimate the importance of not letting the Turks win –

G.O.C. (*quietly*): They won't win.

LAWRENCE: They won at the Dardanelles ... and Kut. And there's Suez – and here we are on the route of England's life-line to the East ... The Turks could cut one of the main arteries of the British Empire – if we let them. And there are the Arabs ... After centuries of merciless repression, in revolt ... Without your help, they'll be smashed. But if you give them the help that the Germans have given the Turks, they'll win! ... They'll be a force that must be of vital use to you, sir – in your campaign ... they may even mean the difference between victory and defeat ...

The G.O.C. *His fingers stroke his cheek, or he toys with a pencil, or some such action. He is considering, deeply.*

G.O.C. (*slowly, judicially*): As far as I can see, there's not much to be lost and a good deal to be gained by trying it.

LAWRENCE: Yes, sir.

The G.O.C. *makes up his mind.*

G.O.C. (*in a quick tone of decision and finality*): All right! I'll see that Feisal has what you promised. I'll send some regular officers up to him with supplies at once.

LAWRENCE: Thank you sir, I ...

G.O.C. (*dismissing him*): Alright. That's all ...

LAWRENCE (*drawing himself up and saluting*): Yes, sir ...

LAWRENCE *moves out of picture. The* G.O.C. *looks up.*

G.O.C.: Oh! ... Lawrence!

LAWRENCE *has reached the door. He turns.*

LAWRENCE: Sir?

He moves back towards the G.O.C. *The* G.O.C. *and* LAWRENCE.

G.O.C.: The Colonel doesn't want you back in his office!

LAWRENCE: No, sir.

G.O.C.: I rather agree with him!

LAWRENCE: Yes, sir.

G.O.C.: You will take these supplies to Feisal yourself, and remain with him, as military adviser –

LAWRENCE. *He is utterly taken aback.*

LAWRENCE: But, sir –

G.O.C.'S VOICE: Well?

LAWRENCE: I should be of no use there.

The G.O.C. *and* LAWRENCE.

G.O.C.: Why not?

55

LAWRENCE: I hate responsibility!

G.O.C. (*dryly*): I hadn't noticed it.

LAWRENCE: I'm utterly unlike a soldier.

G.O.C.: *That* I *had* noticed!

LAWRENCE: Ideas have always meant more to me than carrying them out ... and to have the ordering and disposing of men ... I'm unfitted for it.

G.O.C.: We shall see.

LAWRENCE (*as if that were the last word*): I can't undertake it, Sir.

The G.O.C. *He is too big a man to use his authority direct as he might; but has his own appreciation of the situation.*

G.O.C.: I don't quite know how to deal with you! To give you an order seems – well ... a waste of breath!!! Let me put it this way: you come to me with rather an unusual request: I've granted it. Now I'm making a request of you.

LAWRENCE: Yes, sir ... I'll go.

33. *Wehj. In* FEISAL's *private tent.* LAWRENCE *is having breakfast with* FEISAL. *'An ordinary bell-tent, furnished with cigarettes, a camp bed – and rugs.'* FEISAL, *smoking and sipping coffee, is dictating to a* SECRETARY. *The* SECRETARY, *'a sad-faced person made conspicuous in the army by his baggy umbrella'. Before* LAWRENCE *is a tray of dates, cakes and coffee.* FEISAL's *body slave,* HEJRIS, *hovers – ministering to them with finger bowls and so on.*

FEISAL (*dictating letter, as his secretary writes it down*): 'So, with this my greetings, and hopes that you will come that I may administer the Oath which so many chiefs are taking.'

... Add: 'and the greater the chiefs the more readily they come.'

FEISAL *turns to* LAWRENCE *with a smile.*

FEISAL: That will please him! His tribe and his position are but small!

FEISAL *turns again to his secretary.*

FEISAL (*dictating*): 'Ride as soon as you may: bringing as many men and camels as you can ... For the rest, bring only your own faith, loyalty and courage: we can supply you with all else to make those things effective.'

FEISAL *takes the letter from his secretary.*

FEISAL (*as he signs it*): See that a messenger rides with this at once.

The SECRETARY *takes the letter, and his umbrella, and leaves the tent.*

FEISAL: They come, more of them, and swifter than we could have hoped.

LAWRENCE: But not Auda.

FEISAL: True. Not Auda.

LAWRENCE: Yet, without him, the revolt can be but half a revolt.

FEISAL: I have done all in my power. He will not join us.

LAWRENCE: I never reached Auda's own country. I know of him only by hearsay.

FEISAL: Auda is the greatest fighter of the desert; with the greatest following. But for all his greatness he is a child ... And my father has offended him beyond repair ... First, not to let him know of the revolt – and then when he came of his own free will, to bid the great Auda serve under Chiefs he had defeated in his own Tribal wars ... He sits there in his tent, nursing his wounded pride.

LAWRENCE: He rides away to his own country tomorrow.

FEISAL: Are you sure?

LAWRENCE: His men have orders to march in the morning.

FEISAL: So! ... Our first reverse ... We must go forward with those we have. I wish to ask a favour of you.

LAWRENCE *bows.*

FEISAL: ... The only wearers of khaki the tribesmen know have been Turks. Naturally your presence in my tent is something of a sensation.

LAWRENCE: I understand.

FEISAL: If you will wear Meccan clothes they will accept you as an Arab leader.

LAWRENCE *smiles.*

LAWRENCE: As you wish.

FEISAL: I have some wedding robes which my aunt sent to me from Mecca – (*smiling*) a little hint! (*calling*) Hejris!

34. FEISAL's *encampment. The reception tent. A large long tent – completely open on one side. The whole thing is set as for an official occasion.* FEISAL *is there, surrounded by the full panoply of desert royalty.* LAWRENCE *is near him in magnificent Meccan robes. Included in the group are several officers in British uniform, but wearing Arab headdress. Around them, other Arab chiefs, Arab soldiers and negro slaves.*

35. *The* BEDOUIN CHIEF *rides up towards the reception tent.* FEISAL *rises in greeting. The* BEDOUIN CHIEF *dismounts. And moves towards* FEISAL.

36. *Yet another magnificent-looking chieftain at the head of his followers — the largest group we have seen — approaches the encampment. A long shot of the whole scene. The* BEDOUIN *kneels before* FEISAL.

37. *Away in the distance, the newcomer chieftain and his followers wind their way towards the encampment.*

38. *A closer shot of the reception tent. There is a hush over everybody; and all eyes are on* FEISAL *and the* BEDOUIN.

FEISAL (*administering the oath*): Do you swear to wait while I wait, march when I march; to yield obedience to no Turk; to deal kindly with all those who speak Arabic; and to put independence above life, family and goods?

BEDOUIN CHIEF: I swear it.

The reception tent. The hush is broken. The buzz and hum of talk breaks out again — as after a 'Two Minutes Silence.' And at that moment:

39. *The* SECOND CHIEF *and his followers arrive.*

40. *Among the followers of the* FIRST CHIEF, *the effect is tremendous. Suddenly their faces become suffused with rage and hate ... They scowl and mutter among themselves; and finger their weapons. The* FIRST CHIEF. *He rises to his feet and turns to his followers ... sees the change in them; and looks to see what has made this change. As*

he looks, his face changes. *Close shot of him. His face works con-vulsively in rage.*

41. *The* SECOND CHIEF *and his followers. They are behaving in the same way. The* SECOND CHIEF. *He slips from his mount.*

42. *The two* CHIEFS *advancing in front of their followers who are approaching one another. The followers of the* FIRST CHIEF *watching — The followers of the* SECOND CHIEF *watching —* LAWRENCE *watching. The two* CHIEFS *meet. They confront one another face to face. The hand of one goes to his dagger. Immediately the other grasps his …* LAWRENCE *moves into the picture, between them.*

LAWRENCE: Welcome — (*he addresses him by name*): Had you come a few moments earlier you would have heard — (*he names the other by name*) take the binding oath of Allegiance … 'to deal kindly with all those who speak Arabic; and put Independence before life or family' … You have crossed the desert to take this Oath …

The two CHIEFS *regard this stranger in speechless surprise.*

LAWRENCE: Between you, there can be no quarrel left … You have but one enemy – the Turk.

The two CHIEFS *hesitate. But their hands do not leave their daggers.*

LAWRENCE: I know you both well, by repute. Great names; and of noble descent. And I know that for centuries none of your two tribes have met, without a death to avenge … The greatest blood feud of the desert … Yet, here and now, you have a choice to make – will you destroy each other – or the Turks?

LAWRENCE *has their fixed attention.*

(*He adds, speaking very quietly*) ... Not only every living Arab, but the spirits of those who have died, wait your choice ... they are ready to make their eternal peace. The moment is yours.

The two CHIEFS *grasp hands.*

43. AUDA's *encampment. Obvious and very busy preparations are going on to break camp and move off – groups of Arabs are seeing to the camels – others packing and loading. Others striking their tents. Closer shot of a group thus occupied. One of the Arabs looks up – and whispers to the other.*

AN ARAB (to another): Auda ...

The whisper goes round as they work.

Auda! ... Auda!

AUDA *walking among all these preparations, approaches.* 'He *might be over fifty, and his black hair was streaked with white; but he was still strong and straight, loosely built, sparse, and as active as a much younger man. His face was magnificent in its lines and hollows, haggard, passionate and tragic ... He saw life as a saga; his mind was stored with poems of old raids, and epic tales of fights; he would sing them to himself, in his tremendous voice. He spoke of himself in the third person. He was sure of his won fame; yet with all this he was modest, as simple as a child – direct, honest, kind-hearted, and warmly loved.'* Thus AUDA *walks among his followers. Everywhere they work harder when they see him. Everywhere his approach is heralded by the whisper of his name ... Till it seems to fill the air ...*

Auda! ... Auda!

He approaches his own tent. At the doorway his slaves bow low. He passes in.

44. *Inside are several of his household. His entrance fills them with apprehension. They know he is in a huge sulk, which is apt to flare into a sudden overwhelming rage. In a terrific silence, he stalks to his seat. Timidly they offer him various refreshments. Each time he shakes his head in silence. Finally, with a gesture and exclamation of exasperation, he dismisses them. They are glad enough to retire.* AUDA *sits there alone 'Nursing his wounded pride, and his rage.' The tent-flap is drawn aside and a* SLAVE *shows in* LAWRENCE. AUDA *doesn't move.* LAWRENCE *motions the* SLAVE *to retire. The* SLAVE *retires.* LAWRENCE *approaches* AUDA, *who has not turned.*

LAWRENCE: Auda Abu Tayi ...

AUDA *turns in surprise and regards him, intently.*

AUDA: El Lurens?

LAWRENCE *inclines his head.*

AUDA: I have heard of you.

LAWRENCE: And I of you!

AUDA: What do you here?

LAWRENCE: I was unwilling to let slip this chance of meeting face to face the greatest fighter of the desert.

AUDA *takes a deep breath of satisfaction.*

LAWRENCE (*adds*): Also to learn from the only trustworthy source – your own lips – the reason for your going?

AUDA*'s brow darkens.*

AUDA: Have you not heard?

LAWRENCE: Some idle tale ... of King Hussein; and of your wounded pride – but I knew there was little truth in *that*! ... Auda is too great.

AUDA: What do you know of Auda?

LAWRENCE: What all men tell, throughout Arabia ... and that is much.

AUDA: You have called me the greatest fighter of the desert. I am! Because never do I stop fighting. Always I have a fight with every tribe within reach, so that there shall be no lack of practice. With my own hands I have killed ...

LAWRENCE: Seventy-five.

AUDA (*pleased*): So! ... But never a man except in battle ...

LAWRENCE: Seventy-five Arabs. And of the Turks –

AUDA (*with a great shrug*): Of them I take no account! ... I have been wounded –

LAWRENCE: Thirteen times!

AUDA: And twenty-seven times married.

LAWRENCE (*correcting him*): Twenty-eight.

AUDA *considers: and does some quick arithmetic on his fingers.*

AUDA (*agreeing*): So! Twenty-eight ... And such a man is bidden to serve under his defeated neighbours ...

LAWRENCE: But if you all serve against the Turk ... and your greatness be measured by your service ... none can be above you being the greatest fighter of them all ... Yet if you stop fighting now – now, of all times ... and do not serve at all, you become the least of them ...

AUDA *is taken aback and obviously moved. The persuasive Lawrence is all out to land his fish!*

LAWRENCE: In a few years, you will be eating the fruits of Arab freedom, and not have struck a blow for it yourself ... How will such fruit taste?

AUDA ... *Hesitating. Emotions are sweeping through him. Rage becomes uppermost.*

AUDA: It is not my habit to be questioned, or told my business
– far less by one who is not of our Faith nor of our
People.

Suddenly he shouts out for his SLAVE *by name. The* SLAVE
appears.

AUDA: My guest leaves me.

And AUDA *turns finally away. The* SLAVE *is holding aside the
tent flap.* LAWRENCE *passes through it. The* SLAVE *follows.*

45. LAWRENCE *appears thro' another tent flap ... Entering into*
FEISAL's *big reception tent ... As he comes inside, he stops for a
moment – and looking round him, sees – in medium long shot some
way across the big tent (which is entirely open on one side) – a group
of people: several* ENGLISH OFFICERS; *several* ARAB CHIEFS; *and*
FEISAL. *Closer shot of this group. It is a kind of Council of War.
Military maps are spread out. They all look up as* LAWRENCE
comes into the tent ...

SENIOR ENGLISH OFFICER (*raising his voice a little to speak to
Lawrence off-screen*): ... Hullo, T.E. ... Nobody knew where
you were ... so we didn't wait ... We were wondering
about the next step –

ANOTHER ENGLISH OFFICER: Do you think we ought to
attack Akaba?

LAWRENCE: We must not only attack, but take Akaba as soon
as possible. It is the only Turkish port left on the Red Sea
and the nearest to the railway.

FEISAL (*quietly makes a point that the British will appreciate*): Also
the nearest to the Suez Canal.

The ENGLISH OFFICERS *nod in agreement.*

SENIOR ENGLISH OFFICER (magnanimously): We'll stiffen the Arabs with some regulars –

LAWRENCE: That's a mistake!

The group. LAWRENCE*'s quiet words are a bit of a bomb-shell* ...

SENIOR ENGLISH OFFICER: Really, T.E., you *are* a contrary chap! First you turn up at Cairo with some perfectly fantastic requests – and get everything you want!! ... And now we're offering you more than you could possibly hope for – and you refuse!!!!

Again with these ENGLISH OFFICERS, LAWRENCE *is a subtly and distinctly different person. He answers them with something of their off-hand, slap-dash, slangy manner of talk.*

LAWRENCE: This is an Arab show. Mix in a whole lot of professionals, and you do in the whole spirit of it.

ANOTHER ENGLISH OFFICER: But, *hang* it, Lawrence, surely the Arabs *appreciate* Regular help ...

LAWRENCE: Oh – they would. Very much ... I know Prince Feisal won't mind my saying so ... but if the Arabs know that other people are being paid to do the job for them, they'd do the sensible thing – stand aside, and watch them get on with it!

Broad grins and nods, and appreciative noises from the ARAB CHIEFS ... *An* ENGLISH OFFICER *turns to* FEISAL.

FEISAL (*with a little smile and shrug*): He knows my people.

The SENIOR ENGLISH OFFICER, *and the group round him.*

SENIOR ENGLISH OFFICER: Well ... of course ... if you can take the place on your own.

ANOTHER ENGLISH OFFICER: '*If*'! It's heavily fortified.

LAWRENCE: Not from the North!

SENIOR ENGLISH OFFICER: From the North!!!

Again LAWRENCE *has sprung a bomb. It is* FEISAL *who first realises what* LAWRENCE *means.*

FEISAL: But to approach Akaba from the North ... that would mean a six hundred mile march ...

LAWRENCE (*easily*): That's the idea!

FEISAL *silently motions a slave to bring a map. It is a picturesque Arabian map, mounted on carved wooden rollers.*

LAWRENCE (*pointing to the map and talking with the air of one who knows the country intimately*): Here is where we are now – They've barricaded the front door ... so we go a long way round ...

His finger swiftly traces the route up the map past – Yenbo, Wejh, El Kun, Deraa, Arfaja and curves round to the North of Akaba –

LAWRENCE: ... and walk in at the back. Then ...

SENIOR ENGLISH OFFICER: The thing's hopelessly amateurish!! (*He is very much laying down the law.*) Look here, Lawrence – there's your enemy in force; you attack with a superior force; and put him out of action – once and for all. That's the ABC of the whole thing.

LAWRENCE: It'll cost lives.

SENIOR ENGLISH OFFICER: Oh well ... if you want to fight a war without hurting anybody!

Laughter among the ENGLISH OFFICERS *who are agreeing with their Senior.* LAWRENCE *turns on them. He is roused.*

LAWRENCE: That's what we've got to aim at! That may sound

funny, but it isn't ... (*And now he is laying down the law*). The Arabs are *really* 'volunteers'. They are really fighting because they want to; but they can also pack up and go home whenever they feel like it. That's the difference between the Regulars and the Irregulars.

SENIOR ENGLISH OFFICER (*just a little bit shaken*): ... Yes ... but ... with the place only a hundred miles off ... A six hundred mile march across the desert ... It's ... it's *unthinkable!*

LAWRENCE (*quickly*): The Turks haven't thought of it. That's why they've left the back door, not only open, but unguarded.

FEISAL: And none but Lawrence would have thought of it.

FEISAL *turns to* LAWRENCE.

FEISAL: The march would go thro' Auda's country ... with him it would be possible ... But without him ... (*He makes a gesture of hopelessness.*)

A SLAVE *enters and whispers to* FEISAL — FEISAL *gets up from where he is seated on the ground.*

FEISAL: Come, the feast is prepared.

46. *Close shot of: 'Rice and meat in a great shallow bath five feet across ... brimful, ringed round its edge by white rice in an embankment a foot wide and six inches deep, filled with legs and ribs of mutton till they toppled over ... The centre places were the boiled, upturned heads ... Over this main dish is being ladled out all the inside and outside of the sheep; little bits of yellow intestine, the white fat, brown muscles and meat and bristly skin, all swimming in the liquid butter and grease of the seething scalding fat ... ' The camera moves back to show the slaves ladling all this into the great bath. And further back to show the guests standing in expectant rings*

watching their dinner go into the bath. The ring of guests. Their eyes start from their heads. Their mouths water. 'They utter their satisfaction when a very juicy scrap plops out.' All is ready. The SLAVES *retire. Immediately the first ring of guests, including* LAWRENCE, *the* TWO CHIEFS *of the Blood Feud take their places round the great bath.*

FEISAL: 'In the name of God the Merciful, the loving-kind.'

As FEISAL *is about to dip in the bowl, a slave comes and whispers in his ear. A look of astonishment on* FEISAL's *face. He turns to* LAWRENCE *with shining eyes and repeats the message. Both of them look eagerly to the tent flap which at that instant a* SLAVE *flings back. The* SLAVE *enters and announces with a great flourish.*

SLAVE: Auda abu Tayi!

AUDA comes majestically in. There is silence. AUDA *crosses to* FEISAL *and greets him with the Arab salute.*

AUDA: Greetings to our Lord, the Commander of the Faithful.

The assembled guests watch spellbound. They do not yet dare guess why AUDA *has come to them.*

AUDA: This foreign unbeliever came to my tents talking much of our people. Now I know that every Arab great or small should stand together for our freedom. I would take the oath at your hands.

A hushed murmur of surprise and pleasure runs through the Company. FEISAL *with a gesture invites* AUDA *to sit by his side — so that now* LAWRENCE *is on his right: 'Turning back the right sleeve to the elbow and taking lead from Feisal, they all dip together ...' At top speed they twist, tear and cut and stuff, never speaking; though it is proper to smile thanks when offered a select fragment.* FEISAL *offers* AUDA *a choice fragment which he accepts.* AUDA *bites it then, suddenly he casts it down, spits and cries:*

AUDA: God forbid!

He pulls his false teeth from his mouth and pounds them with his dagger. When they are completely broken he looks up and speaks:

AUDA: Auda had forgotten. Jemal Pasha gave Auda these. Auda was eating his lord's meat with Turkish teeth.

They all laugh as AUDA looks regretfully at the choicest pieces of meat in the dish.

LAWRENCE: Do not despair, Auda. The British Government will send you English teeth.

The group round the table. This group round the bath is absolutely replete. They can hardly lift their hands to their mouths! At a sign from FEISAL, they rise, almost too full to move. To make way for the next ring to take their places – and begin 'twisting, tearing, cutting, stuffing'. Dissolve.

47. *This lot make room for the next … Slaves take up the great bath and bear it outside. They come out with it and are immediately set upon by hundreds of waiting children. They set down the bath – and the children are round it, over it, in it … Outside, the children all stuffed completely full. The bath. Round it, over it, in it are all the dogs of the camp. An Arabian baby, stark naked, sits and gnaws at a piece of sheep's skin. A dog cracks a bone. The great dish – deserted, empty, clean. The feast is over. The moon rises over the sleeping camp.*

48. FEISAL's *tent.* LAWRENCE *and* FEISAL *are still working.* FEISAL's ADC *is at his side. In front of him kneels a* SECRETARY, *taking down an order, and beyond him another reading reports aloud by the light of a silvered lamp which a* SLAVE *is holding. The night is windless, the air heavy and the unshielded flame poised there stiff and straight.*

SLAVE (*reading*): Sheikh Faiz el Ghusein; Nesib el Bekri; Sami el Bekri; Shefik el Eyr and Hassan Sharaf – have arrived, bringing with them 380 baggage camels.

FEISAL *nods gravely as each name is read. The* SLAVE *reads from another paper.*

SLAVE: Talal el Hereidhin sends word that he will meet the army himself at El Kurr –

FEISAL *turns to* LAWRENCE.

FEISAL: Talal has many tribes who wait for us in the North – His help will be invaluable –

FEISAL *rises and goes to the entrance of tent, looks out. He sees, across the valley, the hollows about and beneath, winking with the faint camp-fires of the scattered contingents. He beckons to* LAWRENCE, *who joins him. As they look out, from the distance over the valley, a voice is heard singing.* FEISAL *waves his arm towards the firelights of the army and turns to* LAWRENCE.

FEISAL (*proudly*): We are no longer Arabs, but a people.

LAWRENCE: Without a country – without a capital.

FEISAL: True, but tomorrow you march Northward.

LAWRENCE *does not answer. He looks round and breathes in the night air.*

LAWRENCE: In Northern Syria I once visited the ruins of a palace, built by a border prince for his queen. The clay of its building had been kneaded for greater richness, not with water, but with oil of flowers. I went from room to room, smelling the different perfumes. Jasmine, violet, rose, but at last one of my men plucked my sleeve and said: 'Come and smell the sweetest scent of all.' He led me to a window and with open mouths we drank in the empty, throbbing wind of the desert. 'This' they told me 'is the

70

best: it has no taste.'

FEISAL: It was a Bedouin of the desert who said that. They find a beauty in what we would think empty. They are as unstable as water, washed about like waves before a breeze.

LAWRENCE: One such wave you and I, Prince Feisal, must raise and roll on till it reaches its crest and topples over — at Damascus.

Dissolve to:

49. *Dawn. A ridge on which stands the* ARMY IMAN, *his harsh and very powerful voice calling the army to Prayer.*

50. *The army making preparations for prayer.* FEISAL's *tent.* FEISAL'S IMAN *comes into the picture and, unrolling Feisal's prayer mat, spreads it out in front of the tent. As the voice of the* ARMY IMAN *stops,* FEISAL'S IMAN *begins, crying gently the words of the prayer. His voice contrasts strangely with the harsh, uncultured tones of the* ARMY IMAN. FEISAL *comes out of his tent and kneels down reverently on his mat. General shots of the whole army on their knees, their faces towards Mecca, as the soft tones of* FEISAL'S IMAN *continue.*

51. *Outside* LAWRENCE's *tent. The voice of the* IMAN *can still be heard. On the ground is seated a gorgeously dressed desperado, who should be at prayer. He is festooned with knives and pistols. By his side is a camel saddle with brass cantles and rich engravings.* LAWRENCE *comes through the doorway of his tent and the ruffian holds the saddle up to him.*

THE ARAB: Yours, Lord.

LAWRENCE: Why am I thus honoured?

THE ARAB: I would serve you.

LAWRENCE: How?

The ARAB *hands him a letter which he takes and reads.*

LAWRENCE: You are Abdullah the Robber?

The ARAB *smiles and nods.*

LAWRENCE (*reading from the letter*): Born in Boreida ... Forced to leave the town hurriedly ... Flogged and imprisoned in Nedjd ... Struck a superior officer at Hail ... Killed a man at Medina ... Stabbed a witness in the courtroom at Mecca ... You have served every Arab prince and been flogged, imprisoned and dismissed by them all. You are known throughout Arabia for your habit of fighting with daggers, for your foul mouth and your lies. Withal you are a fine horseman, a master-judge of camels and as brave as any son of Adam?

As LAWRENCE *recites each crime,* ABDULLAH's *smile broadens into a grin, till, at the end, he has a look of proud exaltment on his face.*

ABDULLAH: Even so.

LAWRENCE: And you would be my servant?

ABDULLAH: With my experience, Lord, and my loyalty I should be as your own son to you.

LAWRENCE *turns and looks at the saddle.*

LAWRENCE: It is very beautiful. I ... I accept.

Mix to: ABDULLAH *and two* ARABS *saddling* LAWRENCE's *camel. The expedition for Akaba – ready to move off.* LAWRENCE *is preparing to mount when* FEISAL *comes into the picture.*

FEISAL: I wish I were riding with you –

LAWRENCE: Your place is here; here you have raised your standard; and here the tribes flock to you.

FEISAL: Yet I am anxious. Auda you must have with you.

LAWRENCE: Auda?

FEISAL: Auda must love or hate. You he hates. You made him realise he was behaving as a child – and a very foolish one – he cannot forgive ... And this dual command, with him will not be easy ... To offend him would be disastrous; yet if the others know that he can get his way with you whenever he pleases, you will lose your hold on the tribes ... My heart will be with you.

LAWRENCE (*smiles*): We shall meet in Akaba.

LAWRENCE *mounts his camel and prepares to ride off.*

FEISAL: Peace be with you.

LAWRENCE: Upon you be peace.

His camel rises. The expedition moves off.

52. *Long shot of the winding cavalcade moving across the desert. The cavalcade disappearing over the edge of the desert, going away from us ...*

53. *The desert. Empty. Away on its edge, on the horizon the cavalcade appears, coming towards us. Dissolve: closer shot of the cavalcade.* AUDA *leading – he points, as he sees: away in the distance, a few trees. An oasis.*

54. *The oasis. It is a very small one. A very old* ARAB *is drawing*

*water from a well – to water a very small plot of cultivated ground.
He looks up and gazes out over the desert. He has seen: In the
distance, the cavalcade approaching. The cavalcade arrives. The Arabs
gallop up to a little pool edged with palms and stripping off their
clothes they dive in and swim around in the cool water. The bodies,
black, brown and some almost white with the shadow of the trees
across the water, and the bright patches where their headdresses and
robes are lying at the edge of the pool present a gay colourful picture
which forms a background during the subsequent conversation.*
LAWRENCE *and* AUDA *riding leisurely up.*

LAWRENCE: What is this place called?

AUDA: Kurr. And here is Dhaif-Allah, the hermit of Kurr.

They dismount and AUDA *greets the old man.*

DHAIF-ALLAH: Welcome in the name of God, the Merciful,
the Loving-Kind. But you would be more welcome if you
journeyed with your swords sheathed.

He turns away and walks off, mumbling to himself.

AUDA (*to Lawrence*): He rambles in his talk and recites strange
poetry to his sheep and goats. He does not understand the
glory of war or of fighting. He is mad.

LAWRENCE: It is a madness that makes him seem the only
sane creature in a world of homicidal madmen.

AUDA: Madmen? Is Auda a madman?

LAWRENCE: Not more than the rest of us.

AUDA (*angrily*): Were you an Arab that would be your last
word.

A terrific hubbub off the screen. LAWRENCE *and* AUDA *turn.*

LAWRENCE: Look!

AUDA *looks, his eyes wide with amazement. An extraordinary beast. A cross between a camel and a zebra. It is creating an uproar. It charges out of the picture pursued by an* ARAB.

LAWRENCE: A painted camel!

AUDA: And Abdel Hassin pursues it. (*He roars with laughter*) Someone has painted his camel with many colours ... A good jest! ... I shall make a song of this ... (*He shouts to the pursuing Arab*): Is your camel so little to your liking that you disguise it as a rainbow?

The pursuing ARAB *gives it up and comes to* AUDA.

ARAB: *My* camel? ... It's yours!

AUDA's *whole appearance changes.*

AUDA (bellowing): Mine!! – By the wrath of Allah ... who has done this?

The ARAB *points.* AUDA *looks and strides off.*

55. DAUD *and* FARRAJ. *Two young Arabs. They are scrubbing away at their arms, which are stained to the elbows in dye. Auda striding furiously towards them.* DAUD *and* FARRAJ. DAUD *looks up. His mouth falls open and he bolts like a rabbit.* FARRAJ *is too engrossed with his scrubbing to notice that* DAUD *has gone.*

FARRAJ (*laughing*): Ho, ho – I should like to see old Auda's face, when he ...

FARRAJ *turns to where* DAUD *was and sees* AUDA's *face. He gives a rabbit-like squeal, but* AUDA *has got him. The painted camel. Round it are Arabs laughing their heads off.* LAWRENCE *seated in the shade.* DAUD *and* FARRAJ *run in and squat before him.*

DAUD (*beseechingly*): Auda has ordered my friend a beating –

75

twenty stripes. My Lord will not allow it?

They are immediately followed by the enraged AUDA.

AUDA (*to the boys*): What do you here?

DAUD: Appeal to my lord.

AUDA: There is no appeal against Auda's judgment.

DAUD (*wailing*): Twenty stripes will kill him.

AUDA: One weakling the less.

DAUD: The lord Lurens will not allow it.

AUDA (*finally*): Twenty stripes.

> LAWRENCE. *Here is the predicament of which* FEISAL *had warned him — a very delicate situation.*

LAWRENCE (*quietly*): The lord Auda is just. But the accused may speak. I will hear.

> LAWRENCE, AUDA, DAUD, FARRAJ.

DAUD: Auda boasted there was no camel like his: so when we found the paint, here was the way to make his words true! Together we did it. But I ran away ...

LAWRENCE: Auda has ordered twenty stripes, and twenty stripes there must be. But now the full tale is known, justice demands you should have ten stripes each.

DAUD: Then I may share the beating! Oh, my lord is good and great and kind.

LAWRENCE: What says Auda? ...

AUDA (*grudgingly*): ... So long as there be twenty stripes.

The boys kiss LAWRENCE'*s hand in gratitude.*

56. Night. Round the campfire the Arabs are playing and singing. They have drums, a large wooden pipe and a queer five-stringed zither. Near the musicians is seated an old man who sings in the strange falsetto quarter-tones of Urban Syria. The rest sit round listening and smoking, their strong, gaunt faces like carvings in the flickering firelight. They dance too, a row of men shuffling their feet and clapping their hands in monotonous rhythm, or in a ring, some leaping high in the air, twisting and writhing like men possessed, but ever keeping time with the soberer shuffle of the main body. They are completely lost to the world. Some way off seated on their rugs watching are LAWRENCE, TALAL *and* DHAIF-ALLAH, *and, in another group close by,* AUDA. *The music can be heard all the while in the background and the dancing seen.*

LAWRENCE (*to Talal*): Your arrival today was more than welcome, Talal el Hereidhin.

TALAL: I am eager too to strike my blow for liberty. In the north my people know too well the Turkish rule.

LAWRENCE: Your tribes will help us not only at Deraa, but even farther north at Damascus.

TALAL *smiles and bows.*

LAWRENCE (*continuing*): With the help of English artillery we will drive the Turks out of Arabia.

DHAIF-ALLAH (*interrupting*): What does a man need that he cannot have without killing? Here I grow my food. I am free. I want nothing more.

LAWRENCE: But, Dhaif-Allah, wouldn't you like to know that this garden of Kurr was yours – your very own?

DHAIF-ALLAH (*striking himself proudly on the chest*): But I – I am Kurr.

LAWRENCE *and* TALAL *laugh.*

TALAL (*to Lawrence*): He has as much *love* for freedom as we have –

DHAIF–ALLAH (*half to himself*): Love is from God; and of God; and towards God.

LAWRENCE (*looking from Dhaif-Allah to Talal*): Christianity and Islam are not such strangers.

TALAL: Perhaps. But we both know – and are both fighting for one thing. Freedom.

DHAIF–ALLAH *has been half listening, half thinking to himself.*

DHAIF–ALLAH (*as before, almost to himself*): Love is from God. And God alone is great.

He gets wearily up on to his feet, and shuffles away.

TALAL: Long after we have left Kurr – even after we are in Damascus – the old man will be splashing out the water into his little garden, sure that there will always be travellers passing to buy vegetables from him.

LAWRENCE: He knows contentment in his life – that is much.

Cut to:

57. *Nearby at the wells in the background.* ABDULLAH, *tucking his flowing sleeves about his shoulders, clambers down the well and, hand over hand, they pass up the large leather buckets, singing the while in a loud staccato chant. They empty the water into stone troughs by the well head and the camels bend down their long necks and drink. The men and camels of one tribe are watering. The men and camels of another tribe stand waiting – they cannot get to the wells. An arab chief we have seen before – the* FIRST CHIEF *of the blood feud – comes to a group of those who are waiting.*

FIRST CHIEF (*impatiently*): Why do you wait?

78

ONE OF THE GROUP: Essad's men are at the wells.

FIRST CHIEF: What matter?

ANOTHER: They'll give no room.

The FIRST CHIEF looks round in anger towards the wells ... The other tribe completely surrounds and monopolises them. The FIRST CHIEF and some of his followers.

FIRST CHIEF: Follow me.

He moves towards the surrounded wells, followed by some of his most important men. They make their way, shoving and pushing their way through the crowds round the wells. At the wells themselves. The SECOND CHIEF of the Blood Feud lounges at his ease, watching his men watering their camels, the FIRST CHIEF strides up to him.

FIRST CHIEF: Since when have my people waited like slaves for yours?

SECOND CHIEF: Since the first of your people waited for his Master!

The FIRST CHIEF's hand goes to his dagger. The SECOND CHIEF leaps up, hand on his. They confront one another, like two panthers ready to spring ... Gradually they relax. But immediately the suspense of the last moment seems to be passing, one of the FOLLOWERS of the first chief leaps forward to spit out an insult at his enemies.

FOLLOWER OF FIRST CHIEF: Are your camels so ill-kept and weak that – after a day's march – they must spend a whole night at the wells?

FOLLOWER OF SECOND CHIEF (*leaping forward to answer*): Are your men so feeble that – after a day's march – they cannot wait a brief hour for their watering?

These sallies are greeted by menacing noises — jeers, murmurs, growls from the two tribes.

ANOTHER OF THE FIRST TRIBE (*to the last speaker*): My father killed for a less insult.

ANOTHER OF THE SECOND TRIBE: I know you and your father. He trod softly: the night was dark: and his knife found my father's back.

ANOTHER OF THE FIRST TRIBE: True. Your father never *faced* his enemies.

LAWRENCE: *Alone, sipping coffee: smoking a cigarette and reading, luxury, peace, quiet. Away in the distance, a murmur of many voices. A shot. Silence.* LAWRENCE *lifts his head to listen. The murmur grows. Immediate clamour.* ABDULLAH *the Robber runs up to him.*

ABDULLAH: Come, Lord.

LAWRENCE *rises and follows* ABDULLAH *out of the picture. An Arab stretched on the ground dead.* LAWRENCE *comes swiftly into the picture ... and stops suddenly as he sees the body at his feet. He kneels down: finds the man dead, rises slowly and looks about him. He sees: On one side of him the* FIRST CHIEF *of the Blood Feud with his followers behind him ... On the other side of him, the* SECOND CHIEF *of the Blood Feud, with his followers behind him. An Arab is held captive between two of Auda's guards.* AUDA *himself is near.* LAWRENCE.

LAWRENCE: Who has done this?

AUDA*'s two guards bring their prisoner towards* LAWRENCE. *Immediately a great clamour breaks out among the two tribes.*

FIRST CHIEF: He is ours. His life is forfeit.

SECOND CHIEF: Ours. He must come back to us — unharmed.

80

FIRST CHIEF: If he is not given to us, we shall take him by force.

SECOND CHIEF: We shall protect him with our lives.

The clamour breaks out again. LAWRENCE. *He raises his arms for silence. The clamour dies down.*

LAWRENCE: But this man is dead. Nothing can give back his life. Yet if a life be demanded for his, and a life for that life – the whole fabric of your revolt will unravel. Your freedom that is within your grasp, will perish here, as this man, by your own hand.

Suddenly AUDA *is by his side.*

AUDA: You know not of what you speak. Before ever Turk oppressed Arab, or Arab suffered from Turk was this Feud. A life for a life: blood calls for blood. It is the Desert Law.

LAWRENCE: Madness.

AUDA (*beside himself*): To you our law is madness. To us you are a stranger. But I tell you this: that man (*he indicates the prisoner*) is as dead as he (*he indicates the corpse*). Whatever a foreigner may say, tonight he will die: tomorrow he that slays him, dies.

LAWRENCE *makes a supreme effort for mastery over himself and the situation. He turns to the prisoner, held between the two guards.*

LAWRENCE: Set him free.

The guards let go of him.

LAWRENCE (*to the murderer*): Come with me.

The MURDERER *and* LAWRENCE *move out of the picture.*

The TWO CHIEFS *and* AUDA *look after them — and at each other, completely taken aback by* LAWRENCE'S *behaviour.*

58. *The entrance to a ravine — which shrinks at the end to a crack a few inches wide. The* MURDERER *and* LAWRENCE *move into the picture, so that they are at the entrance of the ravine.*

LAWRENCE: You did this?

MURDERER: Yes, lord.

LAWRENCE: Enter.

The MURDERER *goes into the ravine,* LAWRENCE *follows him.*

LAWRENCE: Make your peace with God.

The MURDERER, *realising now what* LAWRENCE *is going to do, without protest or without any attempt to escape, falls on his knees and begins to pray. He mutters his prayers in Arabic.* LAWRENCE *stands for a few moments — giving him time to pray ... then:*

LAWRENCE: Rise.

The MURDERER *looks up at* LAWRENCE, *realises his last moment has come. His lips cease to move in prayer. In silence he rises to his feet.* LAWRENCE. *He draws his revolver from the sleeve of his cloak, and moves slowly towards the* MURDERER. *The* TWO CHIEFS *and* AUDA: *others of the two tribes in the background. They are sitting silent: nonplussed — A shot rings out. They turn their heads, in amazement, at the sound of it.* LAWRENCE. *He comes away from the entrance of the ravine. The* TWO CHIEFS *and* AUDA. LAWRENCE *comes to them. He speaks to the* CHIEF *of the dead man's tribe.*

LAWRENCE: He is yours — for burial.

LAWRENCE. *There is a numb, dead quality in his voice — as if there was no feeling left in him.*

LAWRENCE: He was not to be saved — I have done my best to save your revolt ... I have taken the burden of his killing on myself: as Auda says, I am a stranger with no tribe. Perhaps you may not count me worthy of your feud.

LAWRENCE *leaves them ... The* TWO CHIEFS *and* AUDA. AUDA *rises.*

59. LAWRENCE *alone in his tent. He is almost in a state of collapse. His hands cover his eyes, as if to shut out the sight and sound and thought of his own deed. The tent flap is thrown back and* AUDA *appears.* LAWRENCE *does not move.* AUDA *comes into the tent.* LAWRENCE *does not move. Quietly* AUDA *sits on the floor.*

AUDA (*very softly*): Lord.

LAWRENCE *does not move.*

AUDA: Now Auda knows that the lord is just. He has done well. He is beyond our feuds. No more blood will be shed but the blood of the enemy.

LAWRENCE *looks up at* AUDA *and smiles.* AUDA *takes his hand and kisses it.*

AUDA (*humbly as a child*): Master.

60. *Cavalcade appearing over edge of horizon coming to camera.* LAWRENCE, TALLAL *and* AUDA *ride at head of column.*

LAWRENCE: Tallal, your men must destroy the telegraph to Akaba and to Cairo. I don't want even Cairo to know when we attack. We ride through the night, occupy the hills above Akaba – and take it by surprise at dawn.

AUDA: Allah be praised!

61. *Insert: Deilan's men destroying the wires. They attach the broken ends of the wires to a camel and drive him off. Surprised by the jangle behind him he gallops off into the desert till the weight of the tangled wires prevents him moving.*

62. LAWRENCE *creeping up the boulder-strewn hillside and arriving at a sniping position at the top of the hill. He sweeps the pass with his field-glasses.*

63. *Turkish troops as seen through* LAWRENCE's *glasses.*

64. *The Savoy Hotel, Cairo.* LAWRENCE's *gorgeously apparelled bodyguard, 'The bed of tulips', all over, daggers, swords and pistols are squatting on the floor. Two British brass hats are striding up and down the corridor. Whenever they pass various soldiers, junior officers and men, they all spring to attention. This becomes comic. 'The tulip bed' show no respect at all these great ones. A* COLONEL *comes in.*

COLONEL (*shouting*): Sergeant!

A SERGEANT *comes up to him and salutes.*

SERGEANT: Sir?

COLONEL: What's all this?

SERGEANT (*as surprised as the Colonel*): Dunno, sir!

COLONEL: Who are they?

SERGEANT: Dunno, sir!

COLONEL: Where do they come from?

SERGEANT: Dunno, sir!

COLONEL: How long have they been here?

SERGEANT: Dunno, sir – wasn't here a minute ago sir –

COLONEL: Well, we can't have them lying about the place, like this –

SERGEANT: No sir.

At that moment, LAWRENCE comes down the corridor. He is in his torn, dirty, war-stained Arab dress; burnt dark by the sun, of course quite unrecognisable as the young Subaltern of the Intelligence Dept. The COLONEL and the SERGEANT.

SERGEANT: Here's another of them, sir ...

The COLONEL turns towards LAWRENCE approaching. As LAWRENCE is passing, he looks up; recognises his old chief; and gives a quick, spontaneous friendly smile, nod and wave – and passes on. The COLONEL's face.

COLONEL (*calling after him*): Here! ... Hullo!! ... Hi! ... You! ...

LAWRENCE *stops.*

COLONEL: Yes ... You! ... Come back! ... Come here!

LAWRENCE *returns. The COLONEL and LAWRENCE.*

COLONEL (*outraged*): What the deuce d'you mean by grinning like that at me?

LAWRENCE: I'm sorry sir!!

COLONEL (*astonished at hearing English*): What's that?

LAWRENCE: I said I was sorry.

COLONEL: You talk very good English.

LAWRENCE: Don't you know me?

COLONEL: Never set eyes on you in my life!

LAWRENCE: Oh yes you have!

COLONEL: That sounds familiar! I haven't been contradicted like that for six months!!!

The COLONEL *peers into* LAWRENCE'*s face.*

COLONEL: ... So it's you, Lawrence. You've turned up again! And about time too!!! How are you?

LAWRENCE: Very well thanks.

The COLONEL *looks at his clothes.*

COLONEL: Gad! You're a real Arab now, aren't you? I'd like to give you a tip my boy – and a word of warning!

LAWRENCE *looks at him.*

COLONEL (*cont.*): Your welcome's going to be a great deal warmer than you expect! I dined with Allenby yesterday.

LAWRENCE: Allenby? What's he doing here?

COLONEL: Oh, he's in command now.

LAWRENCE: That's good news.

COLONEL: I don't know whether you'll find it so good when Allenby learns you've been off in the desert for months without letting anyone know what you've been up to. You've done some remarkable things, my lad. I won't deny that, but you've overstepped yourself this time ... I wouldn't be in your shoes.

The COLONEL *gives a glance down. The camera follows his glance.* LAWRENCE'*s sandalled feet.*

COLONEL'S VOICE: If you had any ...

65. *An Army Council. The* COMMANDER-IN-CHIEF *presides.*
There is a GENERAL *present: and Lawrence's* COLONEL, *a few*
other officers. And LAWRENCE − *still in Arab dress. The*
COMMANDER-IN-CHIEF *is speaking to* LAWRENCE, *rather as a*
head-master to a culprit school-boy, before he gives him a whacking.
And the COMMANDER-IN-CHIEF *is a really big man, his manner*
is terrifying.

COMMANDER-IN-CHIEF: Not only have I been waiting to
hear from you for several months − but −

The COMMANDER-IN-CHIEF *picks up a piece of paper in*
front of him.

COMMANDER-IN-CHIEF: ... I want an explanation of this −

He hands the paper to LAWRENCE − LAWRENCE *takes it;*
and looks at it.

66. *Close shot of the piece of paper. It is an army telegraph form;*
and on it is scribbled in pencil: 'I promise to pay to —— (an Arab
name) when we have taken Akaba the sum of £500 − T. E.
Lawrence.'

67. *The* COMMANDER-IN-CHIEF; LAWRENCE; *and others near*
them.

COMMANDER-IN-CHIEF: Is that a joke?

LAWRENCE: No, sir.

A GENERAL *is next to* LAWRENCE.

GENERAL: May I look?

LAWRENCE *gives it to him. Next to the* GENERAL *is Law-*
rence's COLONEL. *The* GENERAL *and* COLONEL *look at it*
together.

LAWRENCE: We ran short of gold.

LAWRENCE (*continuing*): The Army had to be fed; and kept in the field; this was the only way.

GENERAL: How many of these outrageous things did you issue?

LAWRENCE: As many as were necessary!

Then the COMMANDER-IN-CHIEF *intervenes to ask a direct question.*

COMMANDER-IN-CHIEF: To what amount?

LAWRENCE: About two hundred thousand pounds, sir.

COMMANDER-IN-CHIEF (*icily; into a horribly ominous silence*): Let me see that again.

The offending telegraph form is solemnly passed to him

COMMANDER-IN-CHIEF (*with the form*): 'I promise to pay ... when we have taken Akaba' ... And when will that be?

LAWRENCE: A week ago, sir!

Another LAWRENCE *bomb. Even the* COMMANDER-IN-CHIEF *is taken completely unawares.*

COMMANDER-IN-CHIEF: What's that?!!!!

LAWRENCE: Yes, sir ...

COMMANDER-IN-CHIEF: Heavy casualties?

LAWRENCE: Two.

COMMANDER-IN-CHIEF: It was heavily fortified.

LAWRENCE: I took it from the rear: by surprise.

COMMANDER-IN-CHIEF: You rather specialise in surprises.

1. The celebrated portrait of Lawrence by Howard Coster taken in 1931. Coster told Lawrence that the two people he wished to photograph most of all were him and Gandhi. *The Royal Photographic Society Picture Library*

2. Herbert Wilcox, British film director, and the first to be interested in filming the life of Lawrence. *BFI Stills, Posters and Designs*

3. Rex Ingram, director of the silent classics *The Four Horsemen of the Apocalypse* (1921) and *The Garden of Allah* (1927), amongst others, tried to get a film of Lawrence made but failed. Ironically, Ingram was the prime influence upon David Lean who made his magisterial study of Lawrence in the 1960s. *BFI Stills, Posters and Designs*

4. Alexander Korda, *the* British film producer of the 1930s, who tried for many years to get the life of Lawrence on the screen. *BFI Stills, Posters and Designs*

5. Leslie Howard – the actor most associated with the part of Lawrence. *BFI Stills, Posters and Designs*

5a. LEFT. Korda had discussions with Basil Liddell Hart – seen here with his friend T.E. Lawrence – about using his biography of Lawrence to supplement some of *Revolt's* details. *The Trustees of the Liddell Hart Centre for Military Archives, King's College, London*

6. RIGHT. Korda wanted Lewis Milestone, celebrated director of the anti-war classic, *All Quiet on the Western Front* (1930) to make his film but Lawrence's refusal meant Korda could make no progress for some time. *BFI Stills, Posters and Designs*

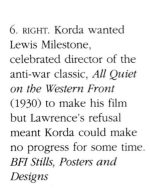

7. Korda next chose his brother, Zoltan Korda, as director. He is pictured here with Korda's star, Sabu, before he travelled to America for the premiere of *The Drum* (1938). *BFI Stills, Posters and Designs*

8. John Monk Saunders, a leading Hollywood screenwriter of the period, was commissioned by Alexander Korda to write the screenplay which Zoltan would direct.
BFI Stills, Posters and Designs

9. Walter Hudd would have been the star of this version. He resembled Lawrence facially. *BFI Stills, Posters and Designs*

F.P.25/-105.

10. ABOVE. Raymond Massey was cast by Korda as Faisal. He is seen here as the Afghan leader Ghul Khan in Korda's *The Drum* (1938). *Jeffrey Richards*

11. LEFT. On the resurrection of the project in 1937, Brian Desmond Hurst was chosen to direct. He is pictured here directing *Prison Without Bars* (1938) for London Films. *BFI Stills, Posters and Designs*

12. A number of leading actors of the period were suggested for the part of Lawrence in the Hurst version. John Clements was one. *BFI Stills, Designs and Posters*

13. Clifford Evans was another. *BFI Stills, Designs and Posters*

14. Yet another was Robert Donat, pictured here whilst filming *Knight Without
Armour* (1937) for Korda. *BFI Stills, Designs and Posters*

15. Laurence Olivier was another put forward for the lead in the version to be directed by Hurst. *BFI Stills, Designs and Posters*

16. In New World Films' plans, James Wong Howe, the great Hollywood camera-man, would photograph the film. He is pictured here working on *Stamboul Quest* (1934) for MGM. *BFI Stills, Designs and Posters*

17. Korda chose William K. Howard as director for what turned out to be his last attempt to film Lawrence. Here William Howard talks with Leslie Howard – who would have again played the lead – at Korda's studios at Denham. *BFI Stills, Designs and Posters*

The GENERAL *and the* COLONEL. *Their minds not working as quickly as the* COMMANDER-IN-CHIEF's. *They are still outraged by the telegraph form; and the news of the fall of Akaba has not altered the situation for them.*

GENERAL: But this unauthorised *flinging* about of money ...

COLONEL: Unheard of! –

The COMMANDER-IN-CHIEF *turns to them.*

COMMANDER-IN-CHIEF (*with just a touch of asperity and impatience at their lack of imagination*): My dear General, you've made two frontal attacks on Gaza – and your casualties?

The GENERAL *is silent.*

COMMANDER-IN-CHIEF: ... More than two? More than two thousand! Considerably. And the cost? Well over two hundred thousand pounds ... And Gaza not yet taken!

The COMMANDER-IN-CHIEF *turns to* LAWRENCE.

COMMANDER-IN-CHIEF: ... Will you dine with me tonight?

68. LAWRENCE *dining alone with the* COMMANDER-IN-CHIEF. *A completely different atmosphere.* LAWRENCE *is wearing an English uniform. He has had a bath; and has taken some trouble with his appearance; he is well-groomed. Fine table linen and glasses. A bottle of champagne. But dinner is over. They are at coffee and brandy. They talk as two equals, in an atmosphere of quiet friendliness. The scene is unhurried; with occasional pauses as they consider and weigh their words; yet, behind it all, the* COMMANDER-IN-CHIEF *is a deeply disturbed and harassed man.*

COMMANDER-IN-CHIEF: The fact is ... the German offensive in France is stripping me of troops.

LAWRENCE: Things over there not going too well?

COMMANDER-IN-CHIEF: ... We're not beaten yet!

LAWRENCE: As bad as that?

COMMANDER-IN-CHIEF: It's an anxious time ...

The COMMANDER-IN-CHIEF *is breaking up his words — taking his coffee.*

COMMANDER-IN-CHIEF: ... I don't suppose there's any one among the Allies, behind the scenes who isn't well ... anxious. And ... I want to be quite frank with you — my position here isn't too easy. Everything must be held up ... not only can I not afford a reverse ... but, as things are ... if the Turks were to attack in force — it might be disastrous ...

LAWRENCE *does not answer immediately. He draws once or twice at his cigarette. When he speaks he gives the impression — however casual his words may be — that he knows what he is talking about; because he has already thought the issues to their source.*

LAWRENCE: There's a passage in Francis Bacon — on strategy ... 'He who commands the sea, may take as much or as little of the war, as he will' ... Substitute 'desert' for 'sea'; a camel is a 'ship of the desert'; and I have a fleet of them ... so I command the desert ... I think I can undertake to carry on our war, here — in a way that suits you.

COMMANDER-IN-CHIEF: More coffee?

LAWRENCE: Thanks.

COMMANDER-IN-CHIEF: Help yourself.

LAWRENCE *does so.*

LAWRENCE (*continuing; in his own time*): An Arab can carry on his own camel, his own food for six weeks. That gives a range of a thousand miles —

COMMANDER-IN-CHIEF: As much as that?! —

LAWRENCE: More — because at a pinch, every man rides on
200 pounds of good meat! I should suggest long-distance
raids on the enemy. Hit him; and disappear before he can
hit back. And then hit him somewhere else while he's still
wondering ... After all, the Turks are Regular Soldiers ...
and Regular Soldiers can't win battles unless they have an
enemy to defeat. We'd never give him an enemy. He'd
never see us: never been anything to aim at ... but he'd
never know where he was going to be bitten next ...
Keep him nervy, and jumpy. He couldn't attack under
those conditions. He'd be all flanks and no front.

The COMMANDER-IN-CHIEF *nods.*

LAWRENCE: I'd suggest raiding their one railway line. I
wouldn't destroy it altogether. I'd keep them busy repairing
it: or trying to guard the whole length of it ... Blow up
a train here, a bridge there ... a piece of track ... We
must not take Medina. The Turk is harmless there. In prison
in Egypt he would cost us food and guards. We must
confine him to the railway in the South. And in the North
—

LAWRENCE *crosses over to the map on the wall and the*
COMMANDER-IN-CHIEF *follows him. As* LAWRENCE *talks*
he demonstrates on the map.

LAWRENCE: I spent a year in Syria before the war studying
the old castles of the crusaders and I know these Syrians.
They are great fighters. With them on the North and
Feisal harassing the railway to the South, you will soon be
in Jerusalem. North of Jerusalem is — Damascus.

COMMANDER-IN-CHIEF: That is the way I had planned it

myself. The capture of Akaba has safeguarded our flank. Now when I am in Jerusalem, can I rely on you to paralyse the railway for me?

LAWRENCE *nods.*

COMMANDER-IN-CHIEF (*continuing*): If you could get behind the Turkish lines and concentrate on Damascus.

LAWRENCE: The moment we get word that you are in Jerusalem, we'll set out for Damascus.

COMMANDER-IN-CHIEF (*knowing that he can trust Lawrence*): Thank you, Lawrence.

They are both obviously pleased that they see eye to eye.

LAWRENCE: Could I have a couple of sergeant instructors from the engineers to teach us about explosives?

COMMANDER-IN-CHIEF: Of course.

LAWRENCE: The art of blowing up trains ought to be worth learning.

COMMANDER-IN-CHIEF: Is there anything else?

LAWRENCE: I shall require rifles, guns, aeroplanes, armoured cars, high explosives ...

COMMANDER-IN-CHIEF (*amused*): Anything else?

LAWRENCE: A battleship to stand guard at Akaba. (*In answer to the Commander-in-Chief's look of astonishment.*) The flagship for preference.

COMMANDER-IN-CHIEF: Just as a matter of interest – why the flagship?

LAWRENCE: In Arabia ships are admired for the number of funnels. Four funnels will impress the Arabs.

COMMANDER-IN-CHIEF: Well, I will do what I can for you.

LAWRENCE: Oh, Sir, one other thing I've forgotten. Very, very important.

COMMANDER-IN-CHIEF: Well?

LAWRENCE: Some false teeth.

Dissolve.

69. *Large close-up of* AUDA *grinning and showing his new gleaming teeth. Pan to:*

70. *A British man-of-war, with four funnels. Lying off Akaba. A group of tribesmen gazing at it.* AUDA *joins the group.*

AUDA: By Allah! ... Now have the British sent us the mother and father of all ships ... of which all others are only foals!

71. *Deck of British battleship.* LAWRENCE *is experimenting with a white box. He cuts a heavy rubber insulated cable in half, and fastens the ends to screw terminals on the box. He joins up a special detonator, pushes down the ratchet handle with the result that the detonator goes off with a bang. Two sergeant instructors of gunnery stand by wistfully watching the operators. One gathers courage to speak. (Note: this scene to be amplified for comedy.) Two sergeant instructors showing some Arabs how to work the electrical apparatus for blowing up trains.*

LEWIS (*the Australian*): Beg pardon Sir, but could you use a couple of gunners against the train?

LAWRENCE: I could.

LEWIS: The sergeant and I would like to go along.

LAWRENCE: But could you stand it?

LEWIS: Begging your pardon Sir – but anything *you* can stand we can.

STOKES: That's right, Sir.

LAWRENCE: Don't be too sure. It's taken me a good many months of hard training ... You'll have to go dry between the wells, as the Arabs do; and, as they say, 'drink deep today for the thirsts of yesterday and tomorrow!'

LEWIS: That's all right, sir.

LAWRENCE: Very well, I will find a couple of camels for you.

Dissolve.

72. *Camel caravan setting out across the desert. Camel caravan marching through desert. The heat is terrific. The air is like a metal mask over the faces of the camelmen.* STOKES. *His face expresses the suffering which he is undergoing.*

STOKES: How goes it Mac?

LEWIS. *He gasps for breath as he rides along.*

LEWIS: ... ma lips are that dry and ma head that hot ... and just when I'm thinking I can't bear another minute of it, I remember the other end of me is so sore that I forget my head ... And just when I'm thinking I can't bear another step of the camel, I remember ma head and forget I'm in trouble at the base!

LAWRENCE *as he rides. His face betrays no emotion. Dissolve.*

73. *Camel caravan arriving at Mudowwara Well.* LAWRENCE *dismounts and approaches well. Well. It is a pool, a few yards square, in*

a hollow valley. Over the face of the stagnant water lies a thick mantle of green slime, from which swell curious bladder islands of floating fatty pink. The stench is overpowering.

ARAB (*to Lawrence*): The Turks have thrown dead camels into the pool.

Expression of utter disgust on the face of the Australian LEWIS.

LEWIS: Dead camels!

STOKES. *His nose is wrinkled in an expression of dreadful distaste.*

STOKES: Crikey! Is this the kind of water you drink?

Group.

LAWRENCE (*filling his water-skin*): It is, when there isn't any other.

LEWIS (*there is a touch of real depth in his words*): I've said more prayers these last hours than I have for the last twenty years – and only for a drop of good pure water – and this is the answer to all ma prayin'! ... the ways o' the Lord are verra strange! ...

STOKES: Gaw' Jock – It's worse than 'aggis!!!

LEWIS *and* STOKES, *filling their water skins and holding their noses at the same time, whilst* LAWRENCE *regards them quizzically. Dissolve.*

74. *Group on brow of hill, overlooking curving line of railway and bridge.* LAWRENCE *and group.*

LAWRENCE (*to* LEWIS *and* STOKES, *who look extremely uncomfortable after their dose of Mudowwara water*): Seems a suitable spot to lay the charge.

STOKES (*pointing*): That ledge would give us a good field of fire.

LAWRENCE (*turning away*): Unload then and set up your tools.

Camels being unloaded and led back to safe pasture. Preparations for blowing up train. The SERGEANTS *are setting up their guns on the terrace.* LAWRENCE *is digging a bed between the ends of two steel sleepers, to hide his 50 pounds of gelatine.* LAWRENCE *laying charge. He gathers up the ballast from the track in his cloak and tips it over the bed of the water course. He covers the charge of gelatine – unrolls the heavy wires from the detonator to the hills – and with long fanning sweeps of his cloak he smooths the sand over the wires all the way from the charge to the firing point two hundred yards off. Group at firing point.*

LAWRENCE: An excellent ambush for the man who fires the charge, except that he cannot see the train approaching. I'll have to give him a signal.

ABDULLAH (*the robber*): Lord, may I have this task of honour?

He is yielded the task by the acclamations of the others. LAW-RENCE *shows* ABDULLAH *what to do on the disconnected exploder. Each time that Lawrence raises his hand* ABDULLAH *bangs down the ratchet handle.* WATCHMAN *on hill. He signals a warning. The Arab riflemen – stripped to their white cotton drawers and love-plaits.* LAWRENCE *and* GUNNERS *drop out of sight.*

75. *Railway. Along the track comes a patrol of forty Turkish soldiers. Although inspecting the line, they walk over the hidden mine without taking notice.*

76. *As the patrol disappears round the curve the watchman on the hill once more raises his hand and calls.*

WATCHMAN: Smoke! A train!

77. *Train from* WATCHMAN*'s angle. It is a long train drawn by two engines. Behind the engines are ten box-waggons packed with Turkish troops, and bristling with rifles.*

78. *Arab* RIFLEMEN *extended in a long line so that they may rake the coaches at close range.* LAWRENCE *watching train through field-glasses. As it approaches the bridge he drops his right arm as he prepares to give the signal.* ABDULLAH *with the exploder on his knees. He dances around crying with excitement and imploring:*

ABDULLAH: Dear God, make me fruitful! Make me fruitful!

79. *Train as seen through* LAWRENCE*'s field-glasses. The roofs of the coaches are covered with Turks in little sandbag nests, their rifle muzzles pointing to either side. The windows and doors, too, are crowded with rifle muzzles. As the first engine passes over the bridge we cut to:*

80. LAWRENCE. *He flings up his arm as the signal for* AB-DULLAH *to fire.* ABDULLAH. *At* LAWRENCE*'s signal he drives the ratchet handle home.*

81. *Train. There is a terrific roar. The railway line and train vanish from sight behind a spouting column of black dust and smoke 100 feet high and wide.*

82. *Out of the dust comes the loud metallic clanging of ripped steel and fragments of iron and plate.*

83. *One entire wheel of the locomotive spins against the sky and*

sails over LAWRENCE's *head, to fall into the desert behind. For a moment following the explosion there is deathly silence, with no cry of man or rifle shot. But as the grey mist drifts away the destruction is revealed.*

84. *The bridge is gone. The front locomotive and waggon have fallen into its gap. Dead and dying are rolled into bleeding heaps against the splintered end. The succeeding waggons are derailed and smashed; the frames buckled. The second engine is a pile of smoking iron.*

85. *The hillside is now alive with shots as the brown half-naked figures of the Bedouins leap forward to come to grips with the enemy.* LAWRENCE. *He runs forward and joins the gunnery* SERGEANTS *on the ledge.* LAWRENCE *traversing the train with enfilade machine-gun fire.*

86. *Train. The long rows of* TURKS *on the carriage roofs are swept off the top like bales of cotton under the stream of bullets which slam along the roof and splash clouds of yellow chips from the planking. The* TURKS *pour out of the far doors to gain the shelter of the railway embankment. They begin shooting from the cover of the wheels, across the rails at the* BEDOUINS *coming down the hillside.*

87. *The ledge.*

LEWIS (*to Lawrence*): It's no good, sir, I can't get at them with the automatic.

STOKES (*grinning*): Here's where I come in.

    STOKES. *He slips his first shell into his mortar, adjusts the elevating screw and fires. The shot falls into the deep hollow behind the train where the Turks have taken refuge.*

88. *Hollow where the trench mortar shell has burst. The place is a shambles. The survivors break out into a panic and rush across the desert, throwing away their rifles and equipment.*

89. *Ledge.*

LAWRENCE (*to* LEWIS): It's your turn again!

The SERGEANT *grimly traverses the desert with drum after drum of machine-gun bullets.*

90. *The open sand beyond the train is littered with bodies as the machine-gun mows down the fleeing* TURKS *driven into the open.*

91. *The valley. The* ARABS, *raving mad, are rushing about at top speed — bare-headed and half-naked, screaming, shooting into the air, while they burst open trucks and stagger back and forth with immense bales of booty.*

92. *Train. The hollow beside the train is littered with booty of all description; prayer rugs, mattresses, flowered quilts, blankets in heaps, women's frocks, clocks, cooking pots, food, ornaments and weapons. To one side stand thirty or forty hysterical women, unveiled, tearing their clothes and hair, shrieking themselves distracted. Without taking any notice of the women, the* ARABS *loot their absolute fill. Each man loads the nearest camel with what it can carry, and shoos it up the valley.* LAWRENCE. *He is rolling up the insulated cable connecting the exploder with the mine. The* TURKISH WOMEN *rush to* LAWRENCE *and fall at his feet with howls for mercy.*

LAWRENCE: Please be quiet. Nothing will happen to you.

ABDULLAH *comes by with his arms full of booty and cries out to* LAWRENCE:

ABDULLAH: An old lady in the last waggon wants to see you.

LAWRENCE, *with his coiled cable over his arm, picks up a cup from the many household goods scattered about – fills his water bottle with clear water from the spouting tender of the engine and starts in the direction of the last waggon. In the end of the waggon sits an ancient and tremulous* ARAB LADY. *Unlike the Turkish women, she maintains her composure and dignity. As* LAWRENCE *enters the carriage and graciously offers her a cup of water she accepts it in puzzled bewilderment.*

ARAB LADY: I am too old to run away. Will death come to me here?

LAWRENCE: You have nothing to fear.

ARAB LADY (*raising her hands in a pitiful gesture of distress*): But what is happening?

LAWRENCE (*gently*): The Turks are using this railway to move troops and stores to Damascus. It falls upon me to hinder the movements of the trains. Unfortunately you happen to be a passenger.

ARAB LADY (*helplessly*): But what will become of me?

LAWRENCE (*easily*): The Turks will be here in a few minutes. They will restore order, repair the damage and undoubtedly you will complete your journey in safety.

ARAB LADY (*as* LAWRENCE *turns to go*): Peace be with you.

As he leaves the old lady he meets LEWIS. LEWIS *has, in contrast to the loot of the Arabs, a strange assortment of 'spoil' in his arms. The train bell, a Turkish fez, a bottle of beer, etc.* LAWRENCE *laughs at him and they walk together along the length of the wrecked train.*

LEWIS: What's the next move, sir?

LAWRENCE: More camel riding, I'm afraid. We'll march North and keep on blowing up the railway line. When we get to Deraa, I want to reconnoitre. It's the strongest place between here and Damascus.

LAWRENCE (*as if it were the simplest thing in the world*): I'll slip into the town and find out where the aerodrome is, how many planes they've got, what the Turkish strength is and the best way to attack and take the place.

They come upon FARRAJ, *wailing in desperate distress.*

FARRAJ (*in answer to Lawrence's questioning look*): Daud is dead.

LAWRENCE (*comforting him*): Take heart, Farraj. There is still much to be done. You shall remain by my side.

93. *A series of shots of train and bridge wreckage all the way up the line.*

94. *A railway station platform, marked Damascus. A train is waiting to start. The front carriage is empty – on it is marked that the seats are free. As the carriages go further back, the prices of seats rise – till those in the last carriage are a fabulous price. Two* OFFICERS, *a German and a Turk, are standing looking at a poster with a picture of* LAWRENCE *on it. A reward is offered – £20,000 for Lawrence alive; £10,000 dead.*

TURKISH OFFICER (*at the poster*): And that will be the end of him!

GERMAN OFFICER (*with the casually triumphant air of one who suddenly produces a staggering piece of news*): It's all over with the Arab Revolt as well!

TURK (*genuinely staggered*): How so?

GERMAN: A Revolution in Russia! ... And the Bolsheviks have made public all the Secret Treaties of the Csarist Government ... And, among them, one between the English and the French dividing up Arabia! ... We've sent it straight to Feisal! He's got it by now ... (*He laughs*): And when Feisal and his chiefs have seen it — they'll not fire another shot ...

He turns again to the poster. The camera moves closer to it.

95. *A hand-bill exactly similar to the poster ... Held by Arab fingers. The camera pans, from the fingers ... to the face of an ARAB SHEIK as he reads it. There is a smile on his lips. An ugly one — a £20,000 look. The camera draws back ... The SHEIK sits with the hand-bill of betrayal in his hands. His SERVANT enters.*

SERVANT: He is here.

> LAWRENCE *appears in the entrance.* FAWAZ *rises.* LAWRENCE *approaches him; the* SERVANT *withdraws.* LAWRENCE *and* FAWAZ. *As they meet; and greet.*

LAWRENCE: Fawaz.

FAWAZ: El Lurens!

LAWRENCE: To what do I owe the honour of this most un-expected invitation?

FAWAZ: I heard that you would pass my village so I sent messengers ... to beg that I might give you entertainment.

LAWRENCE: I am fortunate.

FAWAZ: The fortune is mine, el Lurens.

The SERVANT *appears in the tent-flap.*

FAWAZ (*seeing the* SERVANT): Well?

SERVANT: Your brother.

FAWAZ. *This is obviously a shock; and a bad one.*

FAWAZ: My brother!!

LAWRENCE. FAWAZ. *The* SERVANT.

FAWAZ (*continuing*): What does my brother want?

SERVANT: The word is everywhere, that the Lord Lurens is with you. He comes to pay his homage.

FAWAZ (*his face conveying the exact opposite*): He is very welcome! ... Does he ride alone?

SERVANT: No.

FAWAZ: Who else?

SERVANT: Abd-el-Fair; Ali Kerim; Mohommed-el-Hazaa ...

In an opening in the tent, suddenly – The face of ABDULLAH *the Robber, the Chief of Lawrence's bodyguard.* LAWRENCE. FAWAZ. *The* SERVANT. LAWRENCE *sees the face. It is behind the backs of the other two.* LAWRENCE *moves unobtrusively out of the picture.* ABDULLAH'*s face in the opening.* LAWRENCE *moves into the picture.*

ABDULLAH (*whispering*): ... Master ... We're trapped. Turks ... they surround the village.

LAWRENCE: Wait!

The whole group, watching LAWRENCE *and* ABDULLAH.

FAWAZ: El Lurens!

LAWRENCE *and* ABDULLAH. ABDULLAH'*s face disappears.* LAWRENCE *turns towards Rahmin and moves out of the picture.*

FAWAZ. LAWRENCE *comes to him.*

LAWRENCE: Forgive me. A little trouble with my bodyguard. I have told them I stay here tonight and they must wait.

FAWAZ (*with satisfaction*): Good.

A young attractive-looking ARAB SHEIK *makes a swift and rather flamboyant entrance. He goes straight to* LAWRENCE.

THE NEWCOMER (*making obeisance*): El Lurens.

LAWRENCE: Ali Nazaf.

Then follow other chiefs. Each going immediately to LAWRENCE; *and making obeisance, greets him. And each* LAWRENCE *answers by name. The whole group.*

FAWAZ (*seating himself with a gesture to the others*): Sit.

They sit in a semi-circle.

FAWAZ (*with suave graciousness to* LAWRENCE): So! ... It is not myself, but my family and my people that offer you our hospitality.

LAWRENCE. *He does not know who are his enemies – who his friends (if any) or what may happen at what moment. But this is hidden under an exterior of unsuspecting friendliness.*

LAWRENCE: It is your greatest gift – There is a certain tale –

The others – as they wait. But he dangles them momentarily, on his silence ...

ALI NAZAF (*gently*): ... And the tale?

LAWRENCE. *Story-telling is a pastime of the Arabs. And* LAWRENCE, *who had often sat and listened to such stories, drops now into the consciously dramatic mood of the story-teller. Quietly, without disturbing the atmosphere with his voice, he squeezes every ounce of effectiveness from his tale.*

LAWRENCE: It is of Feisal ... and of the time just before his first revolt ... There was a great review of all your Arab army ... And to this review, came two foreigners – The Turkish Governor, and the Turkish Commander-in-chief ... They were there – alone, unarmed, unguarded – among a people that were not their own ... (*He makes a pause, and looks around him – adding quite naturally*): As I might be with you ... And certain of Feisal's advisers plucked his sleeve, and drew him aside, and whispered in his ear: 'Shall we kill them now?' ... And Feisal would not ... And he would not, for one reason, and for one reason only ...

Again he dangles them. FAWAZ. *His half-closed eyes are full of uneasiness.*

FAWAZ (*as if the question were dragged from him*): ... And the reason? ...

LAWRENCE.

LAWRENCE: They were his guests! ...

LAWRENCE *looks at* FAWAZ.

LAWRENCE: With you, a guest knows not only welcome and generosity, but that he is as safe as in the hands of Allah!

The tent-flap is thrown back. And an OFFICER *of the Turkish Lancers stands in the entrance. The semi-circle breaks. Some of the Arabs scramble to their feet.* LAWRENCE, *whose back is to the* LANCER, *remains sitting. He does not stir. The group.*

LANCER: Where is he?

NAZAF: Who?

LANCER: El Lurens.

Not an Arab flickers an eyelid.

NAZAF: Why should you seek him in my brother's tents?

LANCER (*significantly*): We had word ...

NAZAF: Who told you?

LANCER: A message ... He was to rest here for the night. We have brought the reward, twenty thousand pounds.

Slowly FAWAZ *rises to his feet. But before he can open his mouth* — NAZAF *is speaking again.*

NAZAF: The lord Lurens is not here and if he were, no Arab would betray him for if he did (*he is pointing every word*): ... those nearest him — even were it his brother who loved him dearly — would kill him with his own hand ...

LANCER (*nonplussed*): Whose village is this?

FAWAZ: Mine.

LANCER: What have you to say!!

FAWAZ. *He hesitates. Then* —

FAWAZ (*in a low voice*): ... My brother has spoken for me.

The LANCER *turns on his heel and disappears. The tent-flap falls behind him. The group* — *When he has gone they all turn towards* FAWAZ. FAWAZ. *The group.*

NAZAF: Take him!

Two of them move and seize FAWAZ. NAZAF. *He draws a dagger. And moves out of the picture.* LAWRENCE — *watching, drawn and horror-struck. There is a great cry.* LAWRENCE *averts his head.* FAWAZ. *Stretched on the ground ... And in his hand* — *the crumpled hand-bill ... A reward of £20,000 ... Dissolve.*

96. *Small camel caravan crossing desert ridge.* LAWRENCE *at the head of the troop, riding along with his bodyguard. The caravan comes to a halt.* LAWRENCE *sweeps the desert with his glasses and espies:*

97. *Patrol of Turks marching up the railway line.*

98. LAWRENCE *and his bodyguard.*

ABDULLAH: Let's ride on them!

LAWRENCE: They're not worth it.

ABDULLAH: We can wipe them out!

> LAWRENCE *turns and sees that the temper of his men is to attack the Turks. Finally he nods his head in agreement.*

LAWRENCE: All right.

> *The party splits and rushes forward to take the enemy on both flanks.* FARRAJ. *He rides out alone in front of everyone and does not listen, nor turn his head to the cries of warning.* FARRAJ. *He disappears over the side of the embankment. Thirty or forty shots are fired in the encounter, and the Turks are driven off.* LAWRENCE *galloping up to riderless camel near arch of bridge. Two bodies are lying beside the bridge, one a dead Turk and the other* FARRAJ — *terribly wounded, and with blood welling through his robes.* LAWRENCE *and* FARRAJ. LAWRENCE *kneels beside* FARRAJ *and examines the wound. Two of the bodyguards ride up and dismount. They run to* FARRAJ's *side. The bodyguards take one look at the wound and shake their heads. The bullet has smashed through* FARRAJ's *body and broken his spine.* LAWRENCE *covers over the wound, turns his head and looks up at them.*

ABDULLAH (*softly*): He has only a few hours to live.

LAWRENCE: Help me to move him.

> *An attempt is made to lift him on a camel. The effort seems impossible. For* FARRAJ *has no control over his limbs and cries out in pain.*

FARRAJ: No, no. Leave me alone ... I am dying ... I am happy to die ... I have no care for life ... since Daud died.

Over the soundtrack comes a cry of alarm from one of the bodyguards.

VOICE: Turks!

A patrol of fifty Turks are working up the line towards LAWRENCE *and his tiny party of sixteen. Group.*

LAWRENCE: Help me lift him.

Once more LAWRENCE *and the bodyguard try to lift* FARRAJ. *First in his cloak; then in a blanket. But he screams so pitifully that* LAWRENCE *has not the heart to hurt him more.*

ABDULLAH (*to* LAWRENCE): Lord, we cannot leave him, for I have seen the Turks burn alive our helpless wounded. They will torture him.

LAWRENCE (*turning to his bodyguard*): Get ready to mount.

Turkish Patrol rapidly approaching scene. The bullets begin to sing their spiteful song over LAWRENCE's *head, and to kick up splashes of sand about him.* LAWRENCE *and* FARRAJ. LAWRENCE *kneels down beside* FARRAJ. *His right hand steals into the folds of his robes where he carries his pistol. Tenderly he lifts* FARRAJ's *head.* FARRAJ *opens his eyes and clutches* LAWRENCE *with his hands. A strange, tender smile comes over* FARRAJ's *face as he sees what* LAWRENCE *is about to do. For an instant the old familiar gleam of mischief appears in his eyes as he says softly to* LAWRENCE:

FARRAJ: Daud will be angry with you.

LAWRENCE (*gently*): Salute him from me.

FARRAJ (*as he closes his eyes*): God will give you peace.

By now machine-gun bullets are stinging the air above LAW-
RENCE*'s head. There is a muffled report from beneath the folds
of* LAWRENCE*'s cloak.* FARRAJ*'s body quivers and then lies
quite still in* LAWRENCE*'s arms.* LAWRENCE *eases* FARRAJ*'s
head gently to earth and as he covers his face with his robes:*

LAWRENCE: He was a sunlit being until the shadow of the
world fell on him – the most gallant, the most enviable, I
knew.

LAWRENCE *rises to his feet, turns his back to the Turks, mounts
his camel, and disappears over the embankment.*

99. FEISAL; AUDA; *and other* CHIEFS. *In council. They too are
silent; and their faces like thunderclouds. One of them is reading a
document. He folds it up. And it is solemnly passed back to* FEISAL.
LAWRENCE *enters. They all look at him ... But no one speaks. The
silence is like the great stillness before a storm.*

LAWRENCE (*sensing something very unusual*): I had word that
as soon as I arrived, you wanted to see me.

FEISAL: That is so.

All eyes are on him. Glowering; and silent. LAWRENCE *looks
at them impatiently. His temper begins to rise.*

LAWRENCE: If you have nothing to say to me – I shall go
and rest ... I'm tired; and full of bitterness. One of your
people sought to betray me.

FEISAL: Betray you!!!

LAWRENCE (*raising his voice in exasperation*): Yes. Fawaz – the
traitor.

FEISAL *gives a low short laugh.* AUDA *gives a louder one. A
mocking ripple flows round the group ... Culminating in –*

AUDA: Traitor. *You* speak to us of traitors, el Lurens?

LAWRENCE (*ominously quiet*): Of what does Auda speak?

FEISAL (*suddenly thrusting the document at him*): This!

> LAWRENCE *takes the document, and seating himself, scans it ... As he does so, the anger in his face changes to dismay. The others watch him.* AUDA.

AUDA (*significantly*): Who spoke of the 'Fruits of Freedom'?! And we shed our blood for England and for France ...

> *The* OTHER CHIEFS.

A CHIEF (*with the same bitter mocking*): And the blood that was to wash away our feuds?

ANOTHER: And the fire, that was to weld us into One?

ANOTHER: For independence! ...

> LAWRENCE *and* FEISAL. LAWRENCE *hands the document back to* FEISAL. LAWRENCE. *He gathers his strength.*

LAWRENCE: Listen to me! ... This – (*he indicates the document*) was made before you and I met: I had no knowledge of it. The allies will win – they are fighting for their lives: and however long it may take: whatever the cost: whatever the sacrifice – *they* will not lose ... If you never believe another word I say, believe *that* – for your own sakes. (*He is speaking now in a torrent of passion.*) ... Think of your own people. I ask no more. But judge aright. From the Turks, victorious, you can expect nothing but persecution. From the Turks, beaten, less than nothing.

> *He stops. His strength is spent. A complete silence follows the sharp cessation of his words. In it* AUDA *lifts a warning arm ...*

AUDA: Hark!

The group. 'We listened ... and after a while we heard a creeping reverberation ... like the mutter of a distant thunderstorm.'

AUDA: Guns! Allah help any living thing under that rain.

A silent-footed messenger comes swiftly to the tent: puts a message before FEISAL *and retires.* FEISAL *reads the message.*

FEISAL: They are English guns.

LAWRENCE: English?

FEISAL (*referring to the message*): Yes. Your commander is in the holy city of the Christians.

LAWRENCE (*almost to himself*): Jerusalem has fallen! (*Turns to Feisal.*) Then we must press on. Allenby will send us supplies from Jerusalem! The whole army must march northward – always northward – to Damascus.

During LAWRENCE's *last words a beautiful Arab song rises upon the night air ...* LAWRENCE, *under his breath, murmurs the words of the song in English. It is a love song. Song.*

LAWRENCE: What a mock it makes of violence, of battle, murder and sudden death!

He listens again for a moment to the song.

LAWRENCE: ... tomorrow at this hour, the scent will be as heavy and the stars as bright ... but for many the night is exquisite for the last time ...

(Under his last words, we hear again the ominous rumble of the guns.)

LAWRENCE: Until now I've guided the war thinking always of our men. We've lost very few; and them as it were by accident ... But tomorrow ... tomorrow ... for the first time ... we're part of a military machine ... (*a little pause and then he repeats*) ... Northward ... To Damascus!

Dissolve to:

100. *The army on the march. Now at last we see the whole Arab army on the march for Damascus. First rides* FEISAL *in white at the head of the army, then* TALLAL *at his right in red headcloth and henna-dyed tunic and cloak,* LAWRENCE *on his left in white and scarlet, behind three banners of faded crimson silk with gilt spikes. Behind them the drummers play a march and behind them again the wild mass of bouncing camels of the bodyguard with their pennons, packed as closely as they can move. The men in every variety of coloured cloth and the camels nearly as brilliant in their trappings. There comes a warning patter from the drums and the poet of the army bursts into strident song, a single invented couplet of* FEISAL *and the pleasure he will afford them at Damascus. The army cheers, the drums tap again, the standard bearers throw out their great crimson banners and the whole army breaks together into a roaring regimental chorus. It is a song with a rhythmical beat that the camels love so that they put down their heads, stretch their necks out far and with lengthened pace shuffle forward musingly. Abdel Kerim leads his Gufa men. They are dressed in white, with large head-shawls of red and black striped cotton, and they wave green palm branches instead of banners. – The whole representing a spectacle of unparalled barbaric splendour. An aeroplane swoops low overhead and drops a note. It comes fluttering to earth, suspended from a tiny parachute. The note is brought to* LAWRENCE, *who reads it.* LAWRENCE. *And the Arab leaders, as* LAWRENCE *reads:*

TALLAL: Lord, is it important news?

LAWRENCE: The Turkish Army is scattering. Two columns of six thousand men are retiring in our direction.

TALLAL (*with instant and terrible anxiety*): That will bring them through my own village.

LAWRENCE (*looking at map*): Yes ... It is in their line of retreat.

TALLAL: They must be turned aside.

LAWRENCE: Yes, we must ride for it!

> *They turn away to assemble their detachments.* LAWRENCE. *Racing along the road to Tafas with his camelmen.* TALLAL. *Racing towards Tafas with his horsemen.*

101. *Ext. Day. Village of Tafas. The village lies quietly under slow wreaths of white smoke. It is apparent from a distance that the village has been sacked and burned.* TALLAL. *Riding up to village with his horsemen. Grey heaps of corpses embracing the ground beside the road. From one of these heaps a little child — three or four years old — whose smock is stained red over her shoulder and side from a lance thrust, rises and totters off as if to escape.* CHILD. *She runs a few steps then stands and cries.* TALLAL *flings himself off his horse and stumbles toward the child in the grass. His suddenness frightens her, for she tries to scream and run away, but instead drops into a little heap where she dies. Tallal turns away and remounts his horse. Troops riding along road toward village. Now the roadside is littered with the bodies of old men, women and children. As the troops approach the low mud walls of the village a scene of death and horror meets them. Across the walls, sheep-folds, lie the naked, white bodies of women, nailed there by Turkish bayonets. The smoke from the burning houses casts a merciful veil over the atrocities.* TALLAL. *At the sight he halts his men and turns away.* LAWRENCE. *What he has seen has changed his face into a merciless mask. His eyes narrow into slits and his jaws are fixed.*

LAWRENCE (*grimly to his men*): The best of you brings me the most Turkish dead!

> (*Note. All foregoing scenes are practically obscured by smoke from burning houses, so that they are merely suggested rather than blatantly shown.*)

102. *Retreating Turkish column from* LAWRENCE's *angle.*

103. TALLAL. *His body is racked with sobs as he gazes at the ruin of his smoking village, and the mutilated bodies of his beloved people. He turns and rides to the upper ground and sits for a while on his mare, trembling and staring fixedly after the retreating Turks.*

104. LAWRENCE. *He starts to ride to* TALLAL's *side, but* AUDA *catches his rein and stops him.*

AUDA: Let him be!

105. TALLAL. *Very slowly he draws his headcloth about his face. Suddenly he seems to take hold of himself, drives his stirrups into the mare's flanks and ... bending low and swaying in the saddle, his rifle at his side, gallops headlong right at the main body of the enemy. In his long ride down a gentle slope and across a hollow, the drumming of the hoofs of his mare echoes in the valley.*

106. LAWRENCE *and* CAMELMEN. LAWRENCE, AUDA *and the troops have stopped shooting and sit there motionless – watching the death ride.*

107. TURKS. *The* TURKS, *too, spellbound, have stopped shooting and gaze at the oncoming rider.*

108. TALLAL. *When but a few lengths from the enemy the Arab Chieftain raises himself in his saddle and cries out his war-cry.*

TALLAL: TALLAL! TALLAL!

109. TURKISH REARGUARD. *Rifles and machine-guns crash out.*

110. TALLAL. *Riddled through and through with bullets,* TALLAL's *mare goes down, and the Arab warrior falls dead amongst the Turkish lance-points.*

111. LAWRENCE *and* AUDA. AUDA's *face turns cold and pitiless.*

AUDA: God give him peace; we will take his price.

LAWRENCE (*turning about in his saddle and giving this order for the first and last time in the Arab war*): No prisoners.

> *As the word passes along the line from Arab mouth to Arab mouth – lips twitching with fury and vengeance.*

ARABS: No prisoners.

112. LAWRENCE. *Leading his camelmen in a rocketing charge down the valley against the* TURKS.

113. AUDA. *At the lead of his horsemen, charging down the valley.*

114. LAWRENCE *and his men reach the Turkish machine-guns and turn them on the turks.*

115. TURKS. *Splitting up into three sections and scattering into the desert. A* TURK *drops his rifle and holds up his hands, babbling for mercy.* AUDA *rides him down, whipping three bullets into his chest with his automatic.* TURKISH SOLDIER *on his knees, begging for his life. He disappears under the crashing hoofs of* AUDA's *horsemen.* AUDA *rides up to* LAWRENCE.

116. *Detachment of Germans and Austrians. The only section of the retreating enemy to make a stand is a small group of Germans and*

Austrians. The machine-gunners group around three motor cars and time and again repulse the attack of the Arabs who ride past them like devils. AUDA *gallops into picture, reins up, watches the destruction for a moment. He is joined immediately by* LAWRENCE.

AUDA: Who are those men who fight so bravely?

LAWRENCE: Austrians and Germans. For the first time I am proud of the enemy who has killed my brothers. They are two thousand miles from home, without hope and without guides. Yet their sections hold together in firm rank, shearing through the wrack of Turk and Arab like armoured ships, high-faced and silent. They halt, take position and fire to order. They're glorious.

117. LAWRENCE *and* AUDA *at the head of their men charge against those troops. In this charge* LAWRENCE *is thrown from his camel.*

118. *Ext. Plain. Sunset. The plain is scattered with dead men, animals, horses and an assortment of discarded rifles, machine-guns, field pieces and gun carriages.* LAWRENCE *is lying still dazed and stunned beside his camel.* AUDA. *Coming to* LAWRENCE. *He holds up his leather sword scabbard cut to ribbons.*

AUDA: ... And see!

And his shattered field-glasses.

AUDA: ... And see!

And his pierced pistol holder.

AUDA: My horse shot under me! Six bullet holes through my clothes!

LAWRENCE *and* AUDA.

LAWRENCE: But Auda – you're too valuable to be so reckless.

AUDA: Reckless! ... There was no danger!!

LAWRENCE: No danger!!

AUDA: I can look Death close in the face, but he dare not lay a finger on me.

AUDA *unloosens a little charm that is round his neck.*

AUDA: Many years ago, I bought this. And since, Death has taken my sons, my brothers and very many of my people but always turned from me.

He hands the charm to LAWRENCE, *who takes it in his hands.*

119. *Close shot of the charm – a small amulet of a miniature Koran in* LAWRENCE's *hand.*

AUDA'S VOICE: Much money I paid for it.

LAWRENCE'S VOICE: How much?

AUDA'S VOICE: One hundred and twenty pounds.

LAWRENCE's *fingers turn the amulet in his hand. On the back of it is an inscription: 'Glasgow – 1/6d'.*

120. LAWRENCE *and* AUDA. LAWRENCE, *with a quizzical half-smile, hands back the magic charm. Dissolve to:*

121. *The valley of the Dead Night. The moon shining down on the Turkish dead. In the distance the noises of the Arab encampment can be heard, shooting, singing, revelling, looting.*

122. LAWRENCE *turns with an expression of disgust at the noise*

117

to the bodies, and as we see him straighten the white corpses ... We hear on the soundtrack his own words as in The Seven Pillars of Wisdom.

LAWRENCE'S VOICE: The dead men looked wonderfully beautiful. The night was shining gently down, softening them into new ivory. These soldiers had been very young. Close round them lapped the dark wormwood, now heavy with dew, in which the ends of the moonbeams sparkled like seaspray. The corpses seemed flung so pitifully on the ground, huddled any-how in low heaps. So I put them all in order, one by one, very wearied myself, and longing to be of these quiet ones, not of the restless, noisy aching mob up the valley, quarrelling over the plunder, boasting of their speed and strength to endure God knew how many toils and pains of this sort; with death, whether we won or lost, waiting to end the history.

[*Note: If the treatment of this scene seems unsuitable, we can show* LAWRENCE *arranging the huddled corpses silently. Then, as he hears the sounds of celebrating from the camp up the valley, he murmurs softly to himself:*

LAWRENCE: These quiet ones ... how I envy them.]

123. FEISAL. *He stands on a hillock alone looking out across the plain now littered with the dead bodies of the Turkish army.* LAWRENCE *comes into the picture and joins him. He follows his gaze across the valley; when he speaks it is sadly − almost with a sigh in his voice.*

LAWRENCE: And so the last barrier between us and Damascus is swept away.

FEISAL: Allah be praised we are now near the end of the Arab revolt. Without you, El Lurens ...

LAWRENCE *silences him with a gesture.*

LAWRENCE: This is no time for dreaming, Prince Feisal. We must press on. I want to see Arab rule in the Arab town of Damascus. We must have everything in order before the English arrive.

124. *Ext. Day. The great Gate of Damascus swings slowly open. The cavalcade as seen from the Walls of Damascus. The colourful column with its waving banners and pennons appears to extend into infinity. This is the mighty army which has grown from a tiny group of desert warriors under the leadership of* LAWRENCE. *The Gates of Damascus – side angle. As the detachments pass through the gates and into the historic city we recognise, in turn, the great leaders of the Arab revolt. Nasir at the head of his horsemen. Auda abu Tayi at the head of his fierce Howeitat tribesmen. (The privilege of honourable entry given him for his fifty battles.)* LAWRENCE *in his gleaming white Meccan robes seated in the Blue Mist with* COLONEL STIR-LING. *Past the camera file Bedouin camelmen, Indian Lancers, British Cavalry, Australian troops and a French detachment. Damascus is made with joy over her deliverance from the Turks. Every man, woman and child in the city is in the streets. Householders throw flowers, hangings and carpets in the path of the deliverers. Women of the Harem lean out of the windows of the over-hanging houses, crying and laughing with joy and excitement. They shower flowers on the soldiers and splash them with bath-dippers of scent. The horses of the fierce Bedouins become unmanageable in the noise and shouting of the Damascenes. As* LAWRENCE *rides past in the Blue Mist men toss up their Tarbushes to cheer and women tear off their veils. Dervishes whirl about in front of the car, dancing, howling and cutting themselves. The delirious populace chants the names of the leaders of the Arab revolt.*

VOICES: AUDA ABU TAYI! LURENS! NASIR! SHURRI!

As the Blue Mist arrives at the steps of the Town Hall ...

125. *Steps of town hall, Damascus. The steps and stairs are packed with a swaying mob; yelling, embracing, dancing and singing.* STIRLING *in the uniform of a British staff officer, and* LAWRENCE *in pure Arab dress, make their way up the stairs, the people giving way for them.*

126. *Int. The town hall, Damascus.* LAWRENCE *and* FEISAL *are sitting at a table littered with papers. There is a general air of business with people moving about in the background, telephones ringing, etc. An Arab* OFFICIAL *is standing in front of* LAWRENCE.

LAWRENCE: Water supply? What is wrong?

OFFICIAL: The conduit is fouled with dead men and animals.

LAWRENCE (*writing quickly on a slip of paper*): This, Inspector, will provide you with a Labour Corps working under emergency regulations, who will clear the drains ...

As the Water Department OFFICIAL *departs, the* ELECTRICAL ENGINEER *steps into* LAWRENCE*'s presence.*

LAWRENCE (*looking up*): Ah! I'm glad to see you.

ENGINEER: Is there an emergency?

LAWRENCE: Otherwise you would not be here. The town must be illuminated tonight.

ENGINEER: But for several years now we ...

LAWRENCE: The shining quietness of the first evening of victory will add much to discipline ...

As the ENGINEER *departs the* HEAD OF THE SANITATION DEPARTMENT *steps up.*

LAWRENCE: The streets are full of baggage and corpses. Form a scavenger gang to clear the streets and pestholes. Good-day.

LAWRENCE *turns to* FEISAL.

LAWRENCE: ... My aim is to have Arab government before Allenby arrives. There is still much to do. Sanitation ... Relief work — I have arranged to feed the destitute from the Army storehouses. The Turks destroyed everything they could lay hands on before they left, the fire-engines, the telegraph, the railway station.

LAWRENCE *is obviously tired out.*

FEISAL: You must rest. Go and sleep now. Tomorrow Allenby will be here.

An Australian MEDICAL OFFICER *comes in.*

LAWRENCE: What is it, Major?

MAJOR: The Turkish hospital. It's packed with dead and dying and not a single orderly or doctor doing anything. There are cases of dysentery and typhoid, and perhaps there's typhus and cholera too.

LAWRENCE (*grimly*): I will come.

127. *Ext. Hospital barracks.* LAWRENCE *and the Australian* MEDICAL OFFICER *proceed along the pathway and through the great door of the barracks.*

128. *Hospital barracks — court. Ext. The huge, deserted court is squalid with rubbish of all description.* LAWRENCE *walks around the court and enters a shuttered lobby on the left.*

129. *Lobby. Full shot.* LAWRENCE *and the Australian* MEDICAL OFFICER *step inside. The stone floor is covered with dead bodies side by side, some in full uniform; some in underclothes; some stark naked. There are thirty here, and they creep with rats who have gnawed galleries into them. A few corpses are nearly fresh, perhaps a day or two old, others have been there for long; their flesh discoloured yellow and blue and black. Many are swollen twice or thrice life width, their fat heads laughing with black mouths drawn back from grinning teeth. All are dead. From the vista of a large room comes a faint groan.* LAWRENCE. *Lifting his immaculate white skirt, he treads carefully across the soft mat of bodies whose stiff clothing crackles beneath his feet. As he enters the ward –*

130. *Hospital ward. The dressed battalion of filled beds is so quiet it seems as if these too are dead, each man rigid on his soiled pallet. As* LAWRENCE *and the* MEDICAL OFFICER *pick their way forward between the lines,* LAWRENCE *holding his skirts about him, they hear a sigh and turn to meet the open eyes of an outstretched man, whose twisted lips utter the words:*

TURKISH PATIENT: Pity ... pity ...

Pan camera long with LAWRENCE *as he passes beds holding patients whose hands flutter in pathetic gestures of supplication. Some of them raise themselves for a moment to beg pity and, their strength giving way, fall vainly back upon their beds. The Australian* MEDICAL OFFICER *strides into the scene. He salutes Lawrence – turns his back on the* SERGEANT-MAJOR *and says:*

MEDICAL OFFICER: There are Turkish doctors in a room upstairs, Sir.

LAWRENCE: Take me there.

The two walk off.

131. *A hallway on the top floor of the hospital barracks.* LAWRENCE *and the* MEDICAL OFFICER *are standing in front of a door from which the sound of men's voices issue. The* MEDICAL OFFICER *raps on the door with his knuckles. From the inside comes a burst of excited voices, but the door is not opened. The* MEDICAL OFFICER *raps thunderously on the door with the butt end of his revolver. In reply comes a chorus of frightened jabbering. Since again there is no reply, the* MEDICAL OFFICER *kicks the door with his heavy boot and then backs off and shoots the lock away. He shoves the door open with his shoulder, revolver in hand.*

132. *Room on the top floor. Seven men in nightdresses are sitting about on unmade beds in a great room, boiling coffee.*

LAWRENCE: If you care at all for your personal safety you will be wise to dress immediately, go downstairs, sort out the living from the dead and give me a tally of their numbers.

Without waiting to see their reaction to his words, LAWRENCE *turns and leaves the room, followed by the* MEDICAL OFFICER.

133. *Barracks. A working party of the fifty fittest Turkish prisoners using Turkish tools are digging a common grave in the backyard of the barracks. The* MEDICAL OFFICER *is carrying out the work under* LAWRENCE'*s direction.*

134. *Hospital ward. Stretcher bearers are carrying out the corpses.*

135. *Stretcher bearers. The camera follows a stretcher party in medium close shot as it goes out of the building and returns towards the common grave. The bearers are hardly strong enough to stand up to their work. As the bodies drop in* LAWRENCE *consults his tally-sheet:*

LAWRENCE: Twenty-two ... twenty-three.

Mix:

136. *Ext. Backlot of hospital barracks. Midnight. With the help of flares, which give the scene a macabre aspect,* LAWRENCE *and the* MEDICAL OFFICER *are progressing with their work of burying the dead. All foregoing scenes dimly observed. Mix:*

137. *Ext. Backlot – hospital barracks. Dawn.* LAWRENCE *and the* MEDICAL OFFICER. LAWRENCE *and the* MEDICAL OFFICER *are still carrying on.*

MEDICAL OFFICER (*to* LAWRENCE): That's the lot, sir.

LAWRENCE (*wearily*): Let's cover them with quicklime and fill the pit with earth.

As they begin their labour.

138. *Barrack garden. Bright early morning. The* MEDICAL OFFICER *and* LAWRENCE *are putting away their tools. Their faces are drawn by the all-day and all-night toil, and their dress is soiled and stained.*

MEDICAL OFFICER (*observing* LAWRENCE'S *uncertain mechanical stride*): How much sleep have you had lately?

LAWRENCE: Three hours ... I think.

MEDICAL OFFICER: Since when?

LAWRENCE: Deraa.

MEDICAL OFFICER (*exclaiming*): Deraa? You left Deraa four days ago.

LAWRENCE: (*wearily nods*).

They walk across the backyard of the barracks and into the ward which contains the wounded.

139. *Ward in barracks. The appearance of this ward is entirely different from what it was the day before. The patients have been washed and dressed in clean shirts. Their mattresses have been reversed and Turkish-spoken orderlies stand within hearing. The ward has been disinfected and brushed out.* LAWRENCE, *while the* MEDICAL OFFICER *in the distance bends over a patient, walks through the ward. He is stopped by a British* MEDICAL MAJOR. *The* MAJOR *appears as fresh as a robin. He has a pink, well-tubbed, ham-and-eggs bright early-morning appearance.*

MAJOR (*placing his bulk in front of* LAWRENCE): Do you speak English?

LAWRENCE: If necessary.

MAJOR (*sharply*): You are in charge?

LAWRENCE: In a way – I am.

MAJOR (*bursting with scorn and contempt as he looks about the ward*): Scandalous! Disgraceful! Outrageous! You ought to be shot!

LAWRENCE. *As the* MEDICAL MAJOR *dresses* LAWRENCE *down with all the epithets at his command,* LAWRENCE'*s lips begin to twitch and his drawn, hollow-eyed face begins to work with emotion. Suddenly he throws back his head and laughs full in the* MAJOR'*s face. But the laughter is not normal – it is the wild laughter of one approaching hysteria.* LAWRENCE *and* MAJOR. *The* MAJOR *glares down at* LAWRENCE *with scorn and disgust. He snaps out:*

MAJOR: Wretched little beggar ...

The plump MAJOR'*s tirade is cut short by a wild scream of*

125

laughter from LAWRENCE. *This time his laughter becomes hysterical – wild and uncontrolled. The* MAJOR *slaps* LAWRENCE'S *face and marches away.*

MAJOR: Bloody brute ...

LAWRENCE *and* MEDICAL OFFICER. *That he has finally reached breaking point is indicated by his mad laughter, twisted features and tortured eyes. With a supreme effort he regains control of his breaking mind, and stumbles along the corridor as the* MEDICAL OFFICER *hurries up to his side.*

MEDICAL OFFICER: Let me go after him.

LAWRENCE: What for?

MEDICAL OFFICER: I'd like to boot him out of the place.

LAWRENCE (*dropping down on the foot of an empty cot*): No, no.

MEDICAL OFFICER: But ...

LAWRENCE (*slowly*): After the sand, and the heat, and the lice, and the snakes, and the punishment and the pain ... Do you know that, since boyhood, pain of the slightest has been my secret terror, and yet thirteen bullets have torn their way through my flesh? In the last five actions I have been hit and my body so dreaded further pain that lately I've had to force myself under fire ... you understand, I am not a man of action. I have been hungry, cold; frost and dirt have poisoned my hurts ...

LAWRENCE'S *complete exhaustion is shown by the fact that he can scarcely support himself upright on the cot.*

LAWRENCE: ... For me, sleep was the richest pleasure in the world, and yet sleep has become a stranger to me ... I have known little but wounds, aches, thirst and weariness. Sixty of my bodyguard have found death beside me ...

LAWRENCE *begins to slump into a recumbent position.*

LAWRENCE (*in a detached voice*): The last time I was hit from the air ... and I judged my left arm torn off and began to cry for the pity of it ... it was only a hot splinter of High Explosive ...

By now LAWRENCE *is lying upon the cot, and as sleep takes possession of him he murmurs.*

LAWRENCE (*his voice fading out*): What was it that I started out to say ... Oh, yes, it was about the slap ... Well, what does it matter, now, a little slap in the face ...

As LAWRENCE's *eyes close and his body relaxes into sleep, the* MEDICAL OFFICER, *with a strange show of tenderness, spreads his greatcoat over the white-cloaked figure on the stained army cot. He then takes up a position under the arch at the entrance of the ward.*

140. *Ext. Hotel in Damascus. A grey Rolls-Royce is standing at the entrance.* LAWRENCE *enters the scene with the* MEDICAL OFFICER. *He looks at the grey machine and cries out to the medical officer.*

LAWRENCE: Allenby!

Leaving the MEDICAL OFFICER *he rushes into the hotel.*

141. *Int.* ALLENBY's *suite in the hotel. The great* ALLENBY *is with* CLAYTON *the* CORNWALLIS *and other high-ranking officers, when* LAWRENCE *bursts in.*

ALLENBY (*delighted*): Lawrence!

LAWRENCE: I have established an Arab Government in Damascus with Prince Feisal as Governor.

ALLENBY: Good, I shall confirm it.

LAWRENCE (*directly*): I wish to leave.

ALLENBY (*heartily*): That can be arranged easily.

LAWRENCE: Thank you, General.

ALLENBY: How much leave do you want? Ten days? A fortnight?

LAWRENCE: No, no – I want to be entirely relieved of responsibility – to go away – and never come back.

ALLENBY (*deeply concerned*): You must know that you cannot be spared.

ALLENBY (*shaking his head*): I won't have it, Lawrence, I won't have it.

LAWRENCE (*pleadingly*): My job is finished. I am not a leader. It is for the Arabs to find their own salvation without leaning on an Unbeliever for guidance.

ALLENBY (*stubbornly*): Still I must ask you to remain.

LAWRENCE (*quietly*): This is the first request I have ever made – for myself – leave to go away.

For a long moment ALLENBY *stares down at the little figure in Arab robes standing before him. Suddenly and with a gesture of surrender, he says:*

ALLENBY: How can I refuse you?

LAWRENCE: Thank you. And my last request is that you make me a Colonel.

ALLENBY (*smiling*): Why a Colonel?

LAWRENCE: Because no rank under a Colonel is allowed a sleeper on the train home ...

142. *The station at Damascus. Railway carriage window with its notice 'Sleeper reserved for Colonel Lawrence'. The camera withdraws, discovering* LAWRENCE, FEISAL, AUDA *and behind them,* ABDULLAH. ABDULLAH's *eyes are tragic.* AUDA *is downcast,* FEISAL *is still and quiet. As camera is withdrawing,* LAWRENCE *is speaking.*

LAWRENCE: It is finished now and the job done. Up till now I have never come to the end of anything. I am cured of crude ambition, but am left with a craving for good repute among men. Ah well, I shall try to pick up a new life and occupy myself. I venture to hope that we shall see each other again, but I don't know where I shall live or what do or call myself. I have come to the end of one world and the new world is not yet born.

During the latter part of LAWRENCE's *speech the camera has approached him slowly until quite close to his face. As he says the last sentence he slowly turns his head from camera – and as he does so: Fade out:* THE END.

INDEX